WHAT WOULD

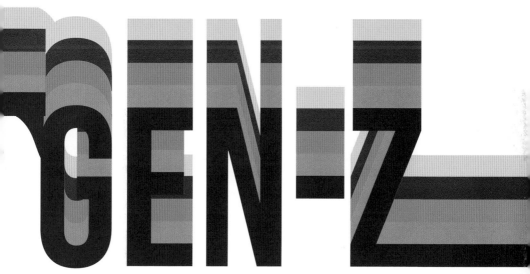

DO?

Published by Familius LLC, www.familius.com
PO Box 1249, Reedley, CA 93654

Familius books are available at special discounts for bulk purchases, whether
for sales promotions or for family or corporate use.
For more information, contact Familius Sales at orders@familius.com.

Library of Congress Control Number: 2022938693

Print ISBN 9781641707367

Printed in China

Edited by Mckay Rappleyea, Sarah Echard, and Shaelyn Topolovec
Cover design by Mckay Rappleyea
Book design by Mckay Rappleyea

10 9 8 7 6 5 4 3 2 1

First Edition

WHAT WOULD

GEN-Z

DO?

EVERYTHING YOU DON'T KNOW
ABOUT GEN-Z BUT SHOULD

JOHN SCHLIMM

Introduction   10

1. If you want to know something, just ask them   14

2. They're really not ignoring you; they're just master multitaskers   18

3. They smash through stigmas and stereotypes by saying the words   22

4. They are the "+" in Compass + Passion = Compassion   25

5. They are each other's greatest support team   29

6. Their tattoos are platforms   32

7. They're not triggered—you are!   36

8. We need to educate ourselves; it's not up to Gen-Z to educate us   40

9. What's up with Finsta accounts?   44

10. That's not modesty; it's the result of being the "Everybody-Gets-A-Ribbon" generation   47

11. They give procrastinators a good name   51

12. They REALLY love their grandparents   54

13. They don't completely understand their Gen-X parents   57

14. They are innovators and inventors thanks to YouTube   61

15. They see their dream goal, but they also know that they have to start on Rung One of the ladder   65

16. Meet them where they are and help them rise from there   68

17. School curriculums need to catch up to Gen-Z   72

18. They are not Millennials   77

Introduction   11

1. If you want to know something, just ask them   14

2. They're really not ignoring you; they're just master   18
multitaskers

3. They smash through stigmas and stereotypes by   22
saying the words

4. They are the "+" in Compass + Passion = Compassion   25

5. They are each other's greatest support team   29

6. Their tattoos are platforms   32

7. They're not triggered—you are!   36

8. We need to educate ourselves; it's not up to Gen-Z   40
to educate us

9. What's up with Finsta accounts?   44

10. That's not modesty; it's the result of being the   47
"Everybody-Gets-A-Ribbon" generation

11. They give procrastinators a good name   51

12. They REALLY love their grandparents   54

13. They don't completely understand their Gen-X   57
parents

14. They are innovators and inventors thanks to   61
YouTube

15. They see their dream goal, but they also know that   65
they have to start on Rung One of the ladder

16. Meet them where they are and help them rise from   68
there

17. School curriculums need to catch up to Gen-Z   72

18. They are not Millennials   77

35. They like to climb on furniture and even rescue trucks, especially for selfies — 142

36. They are still wonderfully prone to mischief — 145

37. They stay up all night, whether you like it or not. So how about a 2:00 am class? — 149

38. They are watching us, especially on social media— so be a role model — 152

39. What would Gen-Z do? — 155

40. Some of them still use paper calendars — 159

41. Research: They have eight-second attention spans. Ummm, only if you don't give them something interesting to actually pay attention to! — 162

42. This approach will fail every time: harassing them, canceling them, and/or giving them lower grades because they disagree with you on politics and other issues — 165

43. Video gamers may rule the world soon, and that's okay! — 170

44. They are studying, and we are preparing them, for jobs that may not even exist yet (and, BTW, undeclared majors are awesome!) — 173

45. They are great listeners, and appreciate when you are honest and vulnerable with them — 178

46. They think nobody likes them, and love to hear that people do — 181

47. The blessing and curse of social media — 184

48. They are marvelously sentimental — 187

49. Just ask them: What does that mean? — 191

50. Many of them carry the weight of the world on their shoulders   194

51. They have exactly what it takes to be future leaders   199

52. Don't try to completely understand them—that's impossible   202

ACTIVITY GUIDE   205

DIY Gen-Z Time Capsules   207

The Blank Sketchbook Project   209

Dear 5-Year-Old Me   211

Dear 85-Year-Old Me   213

It's A Gen-Z World, And We All Just Live In It!   215

The Gen-Z Blackout Poetry Project   217

Pick A Word, Any Word   219

Pick A Topic, Any Topic   221

The Gen-Z Brain Project   223

The Gen-Z Tree Project   225

The Gen-Z Reality Show   227

Name That Generation Game   229

The Planting Truth Project   231

Gen-Z Show-And-Tell   233

The Intersections Of Gen-Z   235

A----->Gen-Z   237

Acknowledgments   238

About the Author   239

About Familius   240

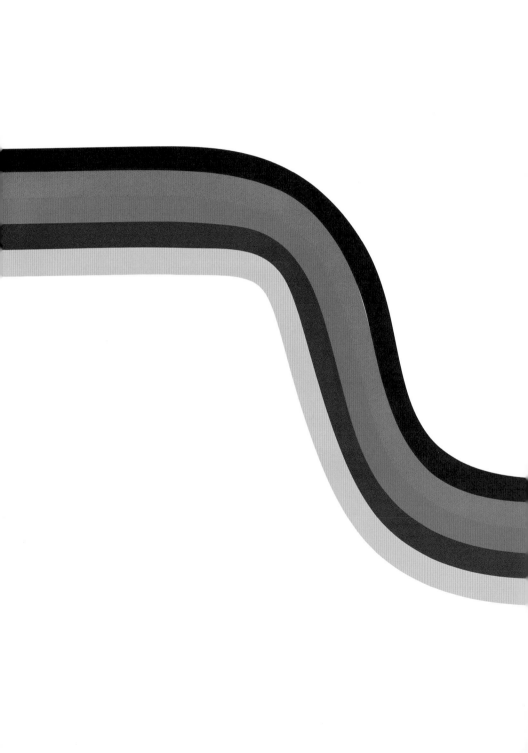

To all the Gen-Zers.

Please consider this book—written for those who live and work and share the world with you—as my gift to you, and my way of saying . . .

I respect you,
I hear you,
and I thank you for being some of my greatest teachers in this life.

A SOCIETY GROWS GREAT WHEN OLD MEN AND WOMEN PLANT TREES IN WHOSE SHADE THEY WILL NEVER SIT.

~ GREEK PROVERB

Introduction

I found early on in working with Generation Z—those born between 1997 and 2012—that, unlike any generation before them, not only do I get to help plant the trees of creativity, courage, innovation, compassion, laughter, resilience, and healing with them, but I also get to enjoy the brilliant fruits and refreshing shade of those same fast-growing, blossoming trees with them, simultaneously and in real time. It's a reciprocal relationship, each of us a teacher and a student in ever-reversing roles. Teaching and learning, and moving forward together.

As someone who lives or works, or simply shares the world, with Gen-Zers, I bet you understand, at least partly, what I'm saying. And, if not, I promise that you will by the time you are finished reading this book. No one person is an expert on an entire generation, especially one that is not their own. Generations are comprised of millions of individuals, whose many different layers are each merely pieces of a more complex and infinitely fascinating puzzle. When I write and speak about Gen-Zers, it's with the understanding that there are no absolutes or everyone fitting into some neat mold.

For many years, I have been actively listening to and getting to know Gen-Zers in my classroom, through my projects such as *The Gen-Z Time Capsule* that I created in collaboration with The Andy Warhol Museum, and during my travels across the country. I have poured those discoveries, which are grounded in what they want you to know about them, into this book. Still, it's all only a beginning, with much more exploration and learning to come.

My goal with Gen-Z—as an educator and advocate—has never been about mastering expertise but rather about gaining a better understanding of them and in the process learning a little bit more about myself.

From day one, these young people captured my heart and imagination through their courage and honesty in openly sharing their very raw truths, especially regarding their journeys with mental health. By confidently and unapologetically speaking aloud words like "anxiety," "depression," and "suicide" and emboldening the rest of us to follow suit, they have already gifted us with the greatest leap forward in mental health advocacy that the world has ever seen.

And it doesn't end there: they are also using their voices to positively and creatively impact issues around race, LGBTQIA+, the environment, animal welfare, food insecurity, criminal justice, income inequality, and so much more, as well as helping to make life better closer to home, for family, friends, and their communities.

But who are the Gen-Zers? What do they think? What are their hopes and dreams? What have been their greatest challenges, and how have they so brilliantly translated that into strength and resilience?

The purpose of this book is to help all of us get to know Gen-Zers better. When we better understand them, we are then able to more effectively help them to lead and enjoy their best lives. Plus, while developing more productive and stronger relationships with Gen-Zers, we soon realize that we also gain more insights, revelations, and pleasant surprises about ourselves.

On these pages, I also smash through the stereotypes, stigmas, and other ridiculous characterizations that hurt and infect and hinder Gen-Zers and all of us. I'm only following their lead here, since they are the bravest warriors I know when it comes to breaking through barriers and bringing clarity and truth into the light.

As you navigate the following chapters, reflection and discussion questions, and activities and projects, feel free to progress straight through or start wherever you wish and jump around. Take what you need from these pages and tailor it to your own experiences with Gen-Zers, and leave behind what isn't useful for you right now. You can always return whenever you need to.

These chapters can be a solo trip or one you take with colleagues and the Gen-Zers in your life. The opportunity for interaction is literally spelled out on every page.

Consider this book and your journey through it as one more flourishing branch of the Gen-Z tree that all of us—together with these young people—are sowing and reaping, and basking in, together. (And if you want to get super literal here, I suggest jumping ahead to The Gen-Z Tree Project activity on page 225.)

ROCK ON! +++++

~ John Schlimm

CHAPTER 1

IF YOU WANT TO KNOW TO KNOW SOMETHING,

JUST ASK THEM

When it comes to communicating with Gen-Zers, this is lesson #1!

They're often politely and respectfully quiet, modest, or even socially anxious, but that doesn't mean they're rude or have nothing to say.

During the time I was a faculty mentor for the Student Athlete Mental Health Awareness Committee that was founded by student athletes on campus, I took the opportunity to ask many, many questions. I'm endlessly curious, and in this case I saw a prime opportunity to learn as much as possible about a new topic for me: the intersection of Gen-Zers who are athletes and mental health.

During our weekly meetings, I would ask questions like:

"How do you cope with losing?"

"How does your coach handle the mental health needs of your team?"

"Are there specific mental health issues that are triggered by certain types of sports?"

"When you're in physical pain, how do you mentally push through a game?"

"What do you think of transgender athletes?"

"For those of you who were small-town student athletes, was there a particular challenge in carrying the weight of town pride on your shoulders, regardless of whether you won or lost?"

"Can you explain more about what you said—that a lot of student athlete wrestlers suffer from eating disorders?"

Every question I posed was answered thoughtfully and honestly, and almost always from personal experience.

Likewise, at its core, *The Gen-Z Time Capsule* that I created in collaboration with The Andy Warhol Museum essentially asks the question: Who are you? To move ever closer to the answer, we asked Gen-Zers to submit photos and videos of significant people, places, things, and activities when it comes to politics and current events, music, social media, fashion, art, innovation and technology, mental health, sports and gaming, animals and pets, and other topics. All to help the world better understand them as individuals and as a generation.

Whatever you're curious about—the interesting tattoo on their arm, their half-shaved/half-blue hair, the Instagram pic of them mid-air on a dirt bike, mental health, race, how they identify when it comes to gender, world affairs, that slang word they just flung past you, you name it—take the first step and just ask them about it.

I promise, they will tell you.

ASK YOURSELF

    " What assumptions have I made about Gen-Zers because I haven't asked them their opinion or to clarify something?

ASK A GEN-ZER

    " Why is it important to you to be honest and open?

CHAPTER 2

THEY'RE REALLY NOT

IGNORING YOU;

THEY'RE JUST

MASTER MULTI-TASKERS

I've learned to strategically pick my battles with Gen-Zers.

It's more important to me to keep an open and honest line of communication going with them than to pick a fight over them tapping away on cell phones, laptops, and iPads, or even going old school by writing in a journal, while I'm teaching or leading a group discussion. For all I know, they might be running a small country or corporation while sitting there, which wouldn't surprise me one bit.

I've also had students knit scarves and sketch during class—they later shared with me that doing so helped them to actually stay more focused in class. Naturally, I then encouraged them to share their awesome creations with the rest of the students, which they enthusiastically did.

Yes, yes, I know! Technically, it's kind of rude, or maybe flat-out rude, to be multitasking like this. And yes, I'd love their focus to be only on me and their fellow classmates, but still.

By carefully navigating this battle for attention, I have learned that no matter how consumed they are with technology or something else, they are still hearing and absorbing everything I'm saying. I've tested this theory on multiple occasions by purposely calling on students who appeared to be totally consumed by their screens or knitting needles and yarn. Each time, without hesitation, they raised their heads, made eye contact, and provided the perfect response.

In fact, I have even doubled down on my students' ability to multitask. At the beginning of one semester, I handed out two blank sketchbooks (see activity on page 209) along with the simple instruction that I would pass them around during every class meeting—for the students to fill in *while* class was happening—throughout the following four months. And nothing was off limits in terms of what they could express in the sketchbooks. By the end of the semester, the experiment was a fantastic success: their ability to multitask was further confirmed and a few hundred more pieces of the Who Is Gen-Z? puzzle fell into place.

" Have I given up on trying to engage in productive communication with Gen-Zers, or even become angry with them, because I assumed they were ignoring me?

" How are you able to focus on so many different things happening around you all at once?

CHAPTER 3

THEY SMASH THROUGH
STIGMAS
AND
STEREOTYPES
BY SAYING THE WORDS

I'm calling it now: the biggest gift that Gen-Z has already given to the world is their raw courage and honesty in speaking aloud words like "anxiety," "depression," "suicide," and so on—usually in reference to themselves.

This is the most significant leap forward the world has ever seen in mental health advocacy and awareness.

The simple act of saying the words, especially when there truly is nothing simple to what lies beneath those feelings and issues, is a growing tidal wave that is smashing through long-held stigmas and stereotypes about mental health, as well as so many other political and social issues—race, LGBTQIA+, etc. In speaking their truths loudly and clearly, Gen-Zers are planting and cultivating change across the globe, which inspired The Planting Truth Project activity on page 231.

This authenticity and frankness by Gen-Zers is also empowering the rest of us to follow suit, especially when it comes to saying "I need help!" and then seeking the healing we need.

Their example emboldened me, as a forty-eight-year-old Gen-Xer, to go public with my own lifelong struggle with anxiety, as well as to speak about my family's long-hushed history of multiple suicides and the ripples thereof dating back several generations.

Time and again, Gen-Zers have reinforced for me that we each have a platform, beginning with our voices and the seeds of truth we plant.

66 Am I comfortable saying words like "anxiety," "depression," "suicide," and so on, especially in reference to myself? Why or why not? Are there any stigmas or stereotypes that I buy into, and even maybe perpetuate, about certain political or social issues?

ASK A GEN-ZER

66 Why and how are you and your generation so comfortable with using words like "anxiety," "depression," "suicide," and so on, especially in reference to yourselves? Are there any stigmas or stereotypes that you buy into, and even maybe perpetuate, about certain political or social issues?

CHAPTER 4

THEY ARE THE "+" IN

COMPASS
+
PASSION
=
COMPASSION

One day, a student approached me before class to apologize for missing the previous class meeting.

"I went with my grandpa to the funeral home to help him pick out a casket for my grandma," he told me. "No one else was around, and I didn't want him to have to go alone."

I always tell my students that I come from a long line of emotional relatives, who easily shed tears of both sorrow and joy, which is actually healthy and great. So this particular student wasn't surprised when he saw my eyes well up as he spoke.

Across the globe, Gen-Zers are standing up for various causes and issues, especially ones that they feel are particularly important to them, all to make their communities, country, and the world a better, more caring and positive place for everyone. Even more specifically, they have mastered grassroots compassion, extending a loving hug or words of encouragement right at home to family, friends, and others who live and work with them.

While in Los Angeles visiting one the country's most famous rescue dog shelters, I struck up a conversation with a young Gen-Z volunteer, whom the organization had recently recognized as the "Volunteer of the Year."

I asked him, "What motivates you to volunteer here?"

With a smile, he replied, "Because I really love dogs, and I just want to help the world to be a better place for everyone."

For these young people, compassion is about combining the direction—their internal compass of talents and dreams—in which they want to head in life as human beings and as professionals with the passion they have for helping other people, animals, and the planet. When this blending of direction and passion occurs, Gen-Zers more fully understand their enormous potential for effecting positive action and change while finding their unique calling and place in the world.

66 Am I compassionate—especially when it comes to the equation of COMPASS + PASSION? Why or why not? What can I learn about being more compassionate from Gen-Z?

66 Where does your sense of compassion come from? And how do you decide where to focus it?

CHAPTER 5

THEY ARE EACH OTHER'S
GREATEST
SUPPORT TEAM

"Each other!" one young woman instantly answered. "We are each other's biggest supporters."

Gen-Zers everywhere have told me the same thing: that they are each other's greatest go-to supporters—in good times and especially in more challenging times. Not necessarily you, not necessarily me (no matter how hard we may try to be there for them), but each other.

Only they can truly understand what someone their own age is going through. And it's important for the rest of us to understand this key element as we formulate our own plans for working with them and trying to help them. Understanding this allows us to recognize both our limits and our best routes in reaching them most effectively, and to adjust accordingly.

Once, when I was doing an installation of *THE SMILE THAT CHANGED THE WORLD (is yours)* at a high school in Connecticut, a student there told me how even with her own struggles around anxiety and panic attacks, she always sleeps with her phone nearby and the ringer on just in case one of her friends—who also all suffer from various mental issues, including thoughts of suicide—needs her.

66 Who do I go to when I need help, especially with my mental health and other personal issues, and why?

66 Who is your go-to person or support team when you need help with your mental health or other personal issues, and why?

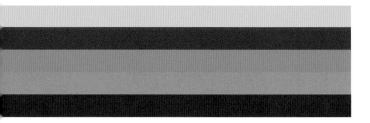

CHAPTER 6

THEIR TATTOOS ARE

PLATFORMS

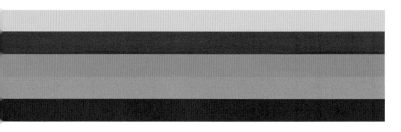

Set aside any negative connotations or reactions you may have to tattoos, and consider Gen-Zers' tattoos as conversation starters.

Ask them the meaning and motivation behind them. You'll likely get a fascinating, even inspiring, earful.

The first time I asked about a semicolon tattoo on a student's arm, she told me that it represents surviving a suicide attempt. Just as a semicolon denotes a pause in a sentence and not an end, likewise the tattoo of one proudly displays that while their life was momentarily interrupted or paused, they survived and went on.

Another student told me that the "X" tattooed on his finger signifies that he is straight edge: no drinking, tobacco, or drugs, abstains from promiscuous sex, and so on. And here I assumed he was just a huge fan of my generation!

I also came to learn that a particularly popular trend with Gen-Zers is having someone like a grandparent's or best friend's signature, or an important date, permanently inked on them.

One student approached me after class and held her upturned wrists out toward me.

"These are the scars from when I slit my wrists," she told me. "I had the scars tattooed so they'd be permanent. Now they are my way of telling my story of survival!"

I don't have any tattoos myself, but Gen-Zers are very close to convincing me to take the leap. If I did get one, I think it would be a ";" on my ankle because as a writer, artist, and advocate the symbolism of the semicolon really speaks to me. Even though I have thankfully never personally struggled with suicidal ideation, I have experienced the pauses that anxiety and other challenges can bring to our lives and the determination it then takes to process, rebound, and forge ahead. And maybe I'd also get an "X" inked on my finger, but in my case as a shout-out to my generation. A cool "Z" and image of the brain somewhere would also fall in nicely with the work I do. And maybe a rescue dog tattoo on my arm.

I guess it's true that once you start inking yourself, you can't stop!

66 What are my thoughts about tattoos—do I like them or think they're awful? Have I ever said, "Why would anyone do THAT to their bodies?" If so, where do those feelings come from? What do my own tattoos signify? If I were to get a tattoo, what would it be, and why?

ASK A GEN-ZER

66 What does your tattoo of _____ mean, and what inspired you to get it?

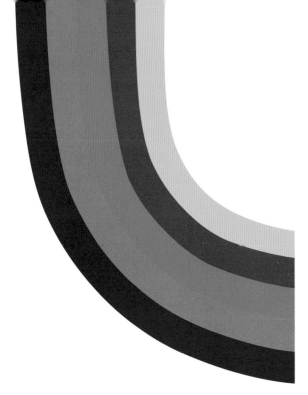

CHAPTER 7

THEY'RE NOT TRIGGERED

YOU ARE!

Part of the stereotype of Gen-Z is that they are easily triggered, constantly complaining, chronically crying about being anxious, depressed, and even suicidal, or plain lazy and detached from reality.

Or that they are "snowflakes" (which is a stereotype originally applied to Millennials).

But the key here is to look past the grossly exaggerated stereotypes, where you'll discover they are not true. Gen-Zers are not easily triggered. They are not a generation of complainers. They are not chronically crying about their issues, nor are they lazy or detached from reality, but rather they're humble and brave in expressing their truths sans embarrassment or hang-ups.

What you will actually discover is that it might very well be you, or other older adults, who are the ones being triggered, complaining, and struggling with mental health and Gen-Z's other issues, not them. You may be the one detached from the reality of what is going on in your own heart and mind.

Among my academic colleagues, parents, and other older adults, I have seen how Gen-Z's openness with discussing their mental health and other issues has triggered many of these individuals, shutting them down in the brain freeze of their own previous traumas.

I once was in a meeting with colleagues who were discussing their first-year students, and it was like watching light bulbs flip on above their heads as they talked, and this revelation dawned on me about these colleagues.

Many of them defensively declared, "I'm not a counselor or psychologist; I'm not listening to their problems! That's not my job!" Or they blatantly chose to ignore what was right in front of them in the classroom as a further defense mechanism to protect themselves: "Oh, nothing is wrong with my students (or my kids); they don't have any issues!"

I could only look at them and think, *If that's how you really feel, then you are in the wrong profession! And, BTW, please get some therapy yourself, so you can feel better.*

66 What about Gen-Z triggers me— makes me annoyed, angry, or not want to listen to what they have to say? And why is that? What happened to me in the past that may be triggering this reaction now?

ASK A GEN-ZER

66 Do you feel that some older adults are triggered by what you may be saying or doing? If so, why do you think that happens?

CHAPTER 8

WE NEED TO EDUCATE OURSELVES; IT'S NOT UP TO GEN-Z TO EDUCATE US

It's not the responsibility of people of color or members of the LGBTQIA+ community, or any other identifiable group, to teach us about (or defend) who they are. When they do, that's a gift they are extending to us.

Likewise, it's not up to Gen-Zers to give us a master class, or even a crash course, about who they are and what makes them tick. As parents and grandparents, teachers, librarians, coaches, community organizers, employers, and others who live and work closely with Gen-Z, it's our responsibility to learn everything we can about them, so that we can help them along their journey. We can also garner our own inspiration and personal growth along the way.

When we actively connect and seek to learn about Gen-Zers—by engaging them in conversations, treating them with respect, and listening to what they are actually saying and not just what we want to hear—they are then more than happy to provide an ongoing master class during which we not only better understand them but we learn a lot about ourselves.

In the sea of incredible Gen-Zers with whom I have had the honor of crossing paths, one of the absolute most brilliant was an African-American transgender man who went on a weekend field trip that I chaperoned to a very famous yoga and retreat center (our trip was generously funded by a grant, and included two other students and one other chaperone).

In the span of forty-eight hours, that young man—whom I had not met before the trip—educated me about transgender living, race, cultural appropriation, the ability to converse with anyone including those who completely disagree with you, his generation, and so much more. He has now become a valued friend, whom I have invited to speak to my other students about diversity in a way that no one else could (remember: Gen-Zers are each other's greatest go-to support team).

Amidst the stunning master class this Gen-Zer gifted me with that weekend, from the moment we arrived, I also closely watched the reactions to our little group by many of the center's other, mostly older and white, guests. There were many glares of judgment, suspicion, and obvious discrimination. I would have liked to have sent this student to the front of the room to speak and open everyone's eyes and hearts to a better understanding of so many things, just like he did for me.

66 How have I learned what I already know, or think I know, about Gen-Z?

66 What are some main things you would like me to know about your generation?

43

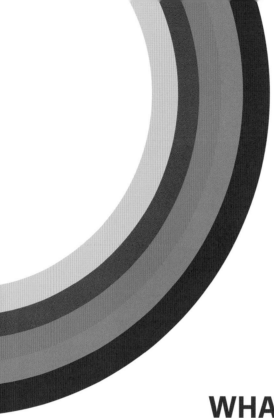

CHAPTER 9

WHAT'S UP WITH
FINSTA ACCOUNTS?

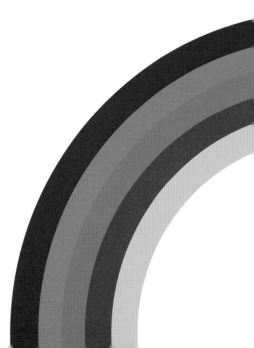

For those of you who might not know, a Finsta is a secret Instagram account, usually hidden under a carefully hard-to-decipher handle. And they are "Invite Only," which likely means you're not invited.

Like me, you have probably thought, *Oh no, what half-naked, booze-filled, career-ending-before-it-even-gets-started photos are they sharing there?!*

But fear not; the majority of Gen-Zers I've interrogated about this very topic assure me that they just use it as a space where they can be their silly, quirky, unfiltered selves as opposed to their official social media pages that are a bit more polished and staged (don't look so shocked—I bet some of you polish, filter, and stage your official social media posts as well).

At one high school I visited, a student told me, "I just use my Finsta to share dumb jokes that only my closest friends will understand or find funny."

Another young woman told me, "My Finsta is where I can just be me, with my closest friends, and not have to worry about how I look or what people will think of me."

66 What assumptions did I make when I heard that young people were using secret social media outlets like Finsta accounts?

66 Do you have a Finsta account? If so, what do you post there, and why?

CHAPTER 10

THAT'S NOT MODESTY; IT'S THE RESULT OF BEING THE "EVERYBODY-GETS-A-RIBBON" GENERATION

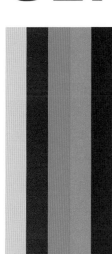

For the longest time, I couldn't figure out why it was so hard to get my students to accept a compliment.

They would tell me about the most amazing things they had done—winning state championships, having poems published, dominating at video game tournaments, performing on major concert stages, earning full scholarships—and I would gush and praise them for those awesome achievements. But they remained straight-faced and noncommittal.

I thought, *WOW! They are so modest!* (Which they mostly really are, by the way, but still.)

Finally, after a few weeks of this quiet "modesty," I was like, "Okay, what's up? Every time I try to compliment or celebrate one of you for your achievements, you look like a deer caught in headlights. Am I just imagining this, or what?"

A young woman answered, "It's because when we were growing up, everyone got a trophy, everyone got a ribbon, just for participating. We're known as the Everybody-Gets-A-Ribbon generation. And we were taught that if we celebrated our wins, it would look like we were bragging and we'd make those who lost feel bad."

AHA!

I thought the everybody-gets-a-trophy-and-ribbon phenomenon was only relegated to the previous upbringing of Millennials, but here I found out that its impact was more serious and extensive than just one generation, and with long-lasting, negative ramifications. For years, many folks working with young people overcompensated in an attempt to ensure no child felt defeated or left out by making sure everyone was celebrated or recognized as a winner. The missed opportunities for facilitating personal growth and cultivating critical thinking skills here—since there will be times when we each win and when we each lose, and learning to understand and embrace both is critical—are now manifesting themselves in the ways I've described above.

I heard this same response from Gen-Zers across the country. Each time I've had this discussion with them, I help them to understand that they can *and* should be proud of their hard-earned individual achievements and wins, and celebrate them, while still remaining modest, of course. And, just as importantly, that they can learn and grow in many ways from their losses and defeats.

66 Have I ever prevented a young person from openly celebrating an achievement or win because I thought it might make the larger group feel bad? Have I ever shielded a young person from loss or defeat instead of helping them to understand it was a learning and growth experience?

ASK A GEN-ZER

66 Have you ever felt like you couldn't celebrate one of your achievements or wins because it might make others feel bad? If so, why did you feel that way?

CHAPTER 11

THEY GIVE
PROCRASTINATORS
A GOOD NAME

Procrastination is nothing new.

I bet some of you even fall into this category that for folks like me—I refer to myself as a recovering control freak and recovering perfectionist—is a scary, dark, heart-racing, anxiety-riddled pit of no return. I still have nightmares where the school bell is buzzing, I have a paper due or exam to take in like two minutes, and I don't have it finished or I forgot to study for it! Oh, and I can't find my classroom!

Deep breath!

Here's the good news: Gen-Zers are helping to blast through the stereotype of the procrastinator as a lazy, uninterested, time-wasting roustabout. (I'm not talking here about the people who simply never finish or never turn in assignments or other work. They give procrastinators everywhere a bad name.)

While many Gen-Zers are like me in getting things done far in advance, I have, in fact, found Gen-Z procrastinators to be some of the most brilliant in the bunch. They just have a different mode of working on assignments and other activities that happens to be very different from mine (I would finish school papers and projects weeks in advance and then fuss over them with edits, tweaks, and polishing until they were actually due).

One Gen-Z procrastinator told me, "This is the only way I can work. If I started on an assignment any earlier than the night before it's due, I wouldn't be able to do it." Just the thought of that makes my pulse race, but he ended up with a dutifully-earned A+ in my class.

My takeaway, thanks to the Gen-Z procrastinators I know: we all eventually reach the same destination if we work at it, but we may take different routes to get there, and that's okay.

66 Am I a procrastinator? If so, what does that mean for the work I do? What is my opinion of procrastinators, and why?

66 Are you a procrastinator? If so, what does that mean for the work you do?

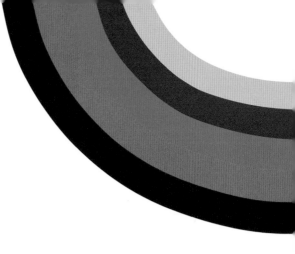

CHAPTER 12

THEY

REALLY

LOVE THEIR
GRANDPARENTS

Gen-Zers LOVE, LOVE, LOVE their grandparents. For many, grandparents were even surrogate or a second set of parents for them.

I mean, LOVE: they have your signatures and names tattooed on their arms, they gush about the time they get to spend with you and the wisdom and love you share with them, and when something bad happens to you, it has a devastating, even paralyzing, effect on them.

One Gen-Zer whom I met was so wrecked by the death of his grandparent that he ended up failing eleventh grade because he missed so much school over it.

Everywhere I go, Gen-Zers tell me the stories of grandparents who are close confidants, adventure companions, and their champions.

So, grandparents, you have definitely earned some bragging rights here!

   Why are Gen-Zers so devoted to their grandparents? Have I seen and heard this among the Gen-Zers I know?

ASK A GEN-ZER

   Are you close with your grandparents? Why or why not?

CHAPTER 13

THEY DON'T COMPLETELY UNDERSTAND THEIR
GEN-X
PARENTS

One of the biggest milestones of my teaching career was when I realized that I was now the age of the majority of my students' parents—a fellow Gen-Xer, born between 1965 and 1980.

This little revelation came after I continually heard about parents who were judgmental, homophobic, close-minded, and so on. Now I certainly know full well that a lot of you parents out there are awesome and doing your best. But hearing my students talk like this suddenly opened an incredible new window through which I could examine my own generation.

Then the light bulb flashed on!

I explained to my students that when their parents' generation were their age, we weren't encouraged—in fact, often we were strictly forbidden to the point of being bullied—to be open about our mental health, sexual preferences, and other issues that were stigmatized as wrong, weird, sinful, and taboo.

I further explained, "But now they have all of you who are so wonderfully open and honest, and not afraid, to say words like *depression, suicide*, and *gay*, and that candor is new for most of your parents. It doesn't excuse anything, but hearing you all be so open could be triggering for them, depending on what they went through at your age without a healthy outlet to express it. Maybe you can cut them some slack and slowly help them to better understand where you're coming from."

I was happy to see nods of empathy and agreement.

To further facilitate a better understanding for all involved, I suggest some get-to-know-each-other's-generation-a-little-better fun. Hop to the end of the book and join your Gen-Zers in creating and playing the Name That Generation Game on page 229 or option number three for either the Pick A Word, Any Word activity on page 219 or Pick A Topic, Any Topic activity on page 221. All three can be easily adapted to focus on only Generations X and Z, or whatever generational mix-and-match combo you'd like.

 Do the Gen-Zers I know understand me and where I'm coming from? Is there any way I can help them to better understand me and my generation, especially in relation to theirs?

 What do you think of other generations?

CHAPTER 14

THEY ARE
INNOVATORS
AND
INVENTORS
THANKS TO YOUTUBE

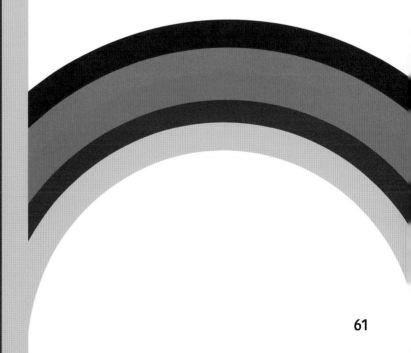

Gen-Zers are fearless innovators and inventors, and until most schools and colleges catch up to them, YouTube and other resources are filling the void.

These young people are using sites like YouTube to learn how to repair cell phones, build computers, play the guitar, fix cars, do astrophotography, and so much more. In many cases, and in a fantastic entrepreneurial spirit, they're learning these skills so they can find work and side hustles to earn money for college and other things.

One student—who sat in the front row of my class, and was always working on his computer or writing in a journal while I was lecturing, but always answered when called on—told me how he and his friend were building a hydroponic device to grow their own vegetables under their beds in their dorm rooms.

"Well, that sounds like it's totally against campus rules," I said with a laugh, "but you are the exact type of person who will one day find the cure for cancer or fly us to Mars, so rock on!"

This kid's eyes lit up, just knowing that for once he wasn't being yelled at or being ushered between his divorced parents' houses but instead was actually being respected and honored for his incredible, out-of-the-box thinking, talent, and ingenuity.

Now is as good a time as any for a little PSA/word to the wise . . . Schools and employers, please take note, and a cue from YouTube: Gen-Zers seek and thrive on skills-based learning to complement their extraordinarily innovative interests and pursuits. Either you need to please adapt and provide it for them or, I assure you, they (and The Imagination Generation, as I call Generation Alpha coming up behind them) most certainly will find it elsewhere, leaving you in the dust scratching your head.

ASK YOURSELF

66 Have I ever talked to Gen-Zers about their innovative and inventive skills, or the related activities or projects they may be working on? If so, did I encourage them to rock on?

ASK A GEN-ZER

66 What projects or activities are you currently working on, and why? And where did you learn how to do THAT?

CHAPTER 15

THEY SEE THEIR
**DREAM
GOAL,**
BUT THEY ALSO
KNOW THAT THEY
HAVE TO START ON
RUNG ONE
OF THE LADDER

Millennials often got a bad rap because, as the stereotype went, they wanted to graduate from college, or not, and stroll right into being the head boss. And some of them have done just that.

Here's where Gen-Zers are like their Gen-X parents. They know the end goal they want to reach—the ultimate dream job, for example—but they also realize that the climb to success begins on rung number one of the ladder, which might mean store clerk, fast food server, gas attendant, nursing home aide, joining the military, or using sites like YouTube to learn a skill.

They dutifully accept this and approach the challenge of attaining a successful life and career with a dedicated ethic.

66 When I was their age, how did I envision my pathway to a successful life and career?

66 How do you plan on achieving your dream goals in life?

CHAPTER 16

MEET THEM WHERE THEY ARE AND HELP THEM RISE FROM THERE

I have long observed my academic colleagues at home and across the country, and I realized that—while the majority of you are for sure awesome, so please rock on!—for many there is still a time-honored, old-school approach: Sitting on lofty, ego-fueled perches of academia, reaching down, and dragging students up to where you are as they are screaming and kicking. A lot of parents, employers, and others also do the same.

If you recognize yourself here, how's that working out for you? Because I can tell you, it's not working for Gen-Zers. Jamming irrelevant or even relevant lessons down their throats because it's going to be your way or no way is not effective. Here's the punch line: they'll just block you out.

Or, to illustrate this another way, one time I was talking to a professor about how he manages his classroom and relationships with Gen-Z students.

He proudly bragged, "I start my class right on the dot, and close and lock the door. If a student is late, even a minute late, too bad—they don't get in."

I took a deep, calming breath, before replying, "But what about if they have a good reason for being late—like a family emergency, road construction, or maybe something came up at their job?"

He firmly declared, "That's too bad, they should then learn to leave earlier if they want to be in my class!"

Eek! All I could think is how I would like to close and lock the door on him, and keep him as far away from young people as possible.

Instead, what works best for all involved is when we meet Gen-Zers where they are and help them to rise from there.

Maybe it's the fact that a student is working a full-time job while going to school or taking care of a sick loved one, and needs some extra time on an assignment. Maybe the most effective way for a student to explore a certain topic isn't via a research paper, but rather in crafting an original video game concept or musical score based around the topic. Or perhaps that particular young person actually isn't being rude, or even shy, by always having their head down and never volunteering an answer—maybe they have social anxiety, and engaging in a one-on-one chat with them will reveal a brilliant intellect and perspective that you never could have imagined was there the whole time.

When we take this productive and much kinder approach, we are all teachers and students in ever-reversing roles, and everyone learns valuable lessons. And everyone rises together!

66 What is my approach to working with young people? Do I meet them where they are and help them to rise from there?

66 What is the best approach that teachers, parents, employers, and others can take in helping you to learn and succeed?

CHAPTER 17

SCHOOL CURRICULUMS
NEED TO CATCH UP TO

GEN-Z

Sometimes it feels like basic school curriculums have not evolved much since the beginning of time—we are still figuratively teaching in one-room schoolhouses.

While there are a growing number of creative and innovative educators and administrators out there for sure (and I applaud you all!), there is still a dry, prevailing format that involves some recipe of textbook, lecture, homework, test, repeat.

Textbook, lecture, homework, test, *blah blah blah*, repeat.

There will always be a place for the right (read: engaging, interesting, speaks to the target audience) textbook and other resource materials, lectures, homework, and (I suppose, in some cases) tests, but Gen-Z is demonstrating, and rightly demanding, the need to flip this pedagogy on its head. Or else the schools will be the ones left behind, because Gen-Zers will forge ahead with or without the rest of us—as evidenced by the number of young people choosing options other than college after high school.

Gen-Zers thrive in discussions, not boring lectures. They want skills-based instruction—hands-on experience that they can actually use in their lives and future careers, not endless formulas, theories, obscure facts, and other busy work that they will *maybe* study and memorize just to get through the test or term paper and then quickly forget. As educators, this dynamic then becomes our fail, not theirs.

Years ago, I told the chair of the Communication and the Arts division at our university that the only way I would agree to continue teaching the Introduction to Public Relations course was if I could get rid of the boring textbook altogether and transform the class into a skills-based experience. As in, the students would walk away at the end of the semester both knowing how to, and actually having crafted things like press releases, pitch letters, proposals, meeting agendas, speeches, PR campaign strategies, social media campaigns, résumés, and other promotional materials, along with developing their critical thinking skills around how PR is at work in every current event they see. As opposed to hearing four months of lectures about the history of PR and endless theories and formulas, and then having to take tests that I myself, as a previous PR major in undergrad and former publicist, would have failed. Our chair readily agreed, and the new skills-focused version of the course was a great success.

More recently, I felt like I was floating on cloud nine during a tour of a high school in Maryland where an entire wing is dedicated to hands-on, skills-based learning: construction, culinary arts, cosmetology, horticulture, nurse assisting, firefighting, informational technology, manufacturing, collision repair and automotive technology, and other options. (This all made me want to re-enroll in high school right then and there!)

This feeling was likewise matched when I saw the skills-focused program at a high school in Montana using The Kindness Rocks & Smiles Community Project™ Art Mural Kit that I co-created with The Kindness Rocks Project founder Megan Murphy. They incorporated the Kit into their efforts to thoughtfully and creatively engage the students there in a hands-on pathway to better understanding who they are and what they're capable of accomplishing in life. And in my own hometown of St. Marys, PA, the local public high school has developed a spectacular training-to-career program that both provides students with hands-on manufacturing skills and gives them incredible opportunities to work with local companies.

Students today also learn more from meeting interesting people, visiting places, and their experiences, and the world around them, than from textbooks and traditional classroom lessons. I always tell my students, "If I know and have access to someone, then that means you do, too."

Over the years, and thanks to the new Zoom Era where almost everyone everywhere is accessible, my guest speakers in class have included a Hollywood producer, a co-host of a popular daytime talk show, the founder of one of the largest interactive and participatory community art projects in the world, a star from a top-rated TV reality competition series, mental health experts, my own literary agent, political figures, a music DJ, pioneering figures in hospitality and tourism, authors, marketing/PR luminaries, grassroots and national humanitarians, arts and humanities leaders, a criminal justice expert, and a number of others who have excelled in their respective fields.

Gen-Zers don't waste brain space or energy on things that they deem useless to them. So we need to decide: Do we remain stubborn and stick to the status quo models of education? Or do we do our jobs and rock-and-roll with the times, and catch up to where our students are and then all rise from there together?

To further kick-start this academic revolution, I suggest checking out the Activity Guide starting on page 205 and consider adapting some of the activities and projects to the work you are doing with your Gen-Zers.

ASK YOURSELF

❝ What do I think of the current ways that schools are educating students? What is my own philosophy or pedagogy when it comes to educating and inspiring young people?

ASK A GEN-ZER

❝ What is the best way in which you learn? How can schools and other places help you to better learn and succeed?

THEY
ARE NOT

MILLENNIALS

Disclaimer: I also loved being in the classroom and working with Millennials.

In fact, I did an entire book—*Stand Up!: 75 Young Activists Who Rock the World, And How You Can, Too!*—celebrating the amazing work they were doing around the world. And I got to deliver my first university commencement address to Millennials, which was titled "The Road to YES Is Paved with Many NOs."

Probably more than any other generation coming of age, Millennials were really slammed with stereotypes and became easy punch lines: snowflakes, too opinionated, think they can just walk right into the boss's job out of college, and so on. These were largely unfair characterizations, and signified how, just like Gen-Zers, they were often misunderstood.

When I walked into my classroom that was filled with the first wave of Gen-Z to arrive on campus, I had never heard the term. I thought we were still in The Land of Millennials. When I playfully referred to them as Millennials, the reaction was swift: "We are not Millennials!"

Oh! I paused for a moment, and finally asked, "Then who are you?"

"We're Generation Z!"

From that moment forward, I've never stopped asking questions and learning who they are, and being their #1 fan.

The underlying issue here is that, like me in the beginning, many people have not yet heard of Gen-Z and so lump them in with Millennials.

Duly noted: it's enough that they have to deal with the onslaught of their own stigmas and stereotypes and punch lines, so they are determined not to also be mislabeled with the misguided shade and quirks of another generation.

66 When did I first hear the term Generation Z, and what did I think?

ASK A GEN-ZER

66 Do you think people still confuse your generation with Millennials? If so, how does that make you feel?

CHAPTER 19

THEY ARE NOT BURNING DOWN CAMPUSES AND DESTROYING CITIES

This should go without saying, but I'll say it anyway, just to be super clear for anyone who needs to hear it.

While Gen-Zers fantastically speak their minds about the issues and causes most important to them, and choose to live authentically and unapologetically imperfect lives, they are not running rampant, destroying campuses and cities in protest.

There will always be extreme and even radical individuals and groups within every generation—including Gen-Z and your own generation—who will be fiercely grounded in political and other beliefs and ideologies. But those extreme ends of any generation or spectrum of belief should never define the whole.

" Have I ever mischaracterized a group of young people as all radical and even destructive? If so, why?

" Do you think people see your generation as radical, and even destructive? If so, why? And, if so, how does that make you feel?

CHAPTER 20

BY AGES SEVENTEEN, EIGHTEEN, AND NINETEEN, THEY HAVE ALREADY STARTED TO TRANSFORM

TRAUMA INTO

STRENGTH

From the very first essays and presentations I assigned, my original wave of Gen-Z students onward have told me about their anxiety, depression, fears, struggles with sexuality, addictions, bullying, miscarriages, eating disorders, abuse, cutting, rapes, disabilities, encounters with racism, seeing friends gunned down, having to get jobs as their family's main breadwinners, and surviving cancer, as well as the parents, coaches, and teachers who have berated them as "too dumb," "too lazy," or "worthless."

For one assignment, I asked my First Year Seminar students to choose a word that had some significance to them and then explore that word in an essay and presentation. A mixed-race student powerfully wrote and then explained from the podium how a certain word had been weaponized against her throughout her life as a racial slur.

I sat transfixed and gratefully better informed, as did her fellow classmates.

Not only did we witness courage and resilience within this presentation, but we were also treated to a glimpse of an extraordinary future embodied in a young woman who once told me that she wants to someday be a US Senator, and no doubt will be if that's where life leads her. In the meantime, I told her that her essay and presentation were literally akin to a masterful book concept pitch around the gravity of a single word and its larger connotation—much like the book Professor Randall Kennedy wrote in 2002 while I was a grad student at Harvard. To this day, I continue to encourage her to bring this impactful page-turner to fruition to further inform us all.

My students, and the Gen-Zers I meet across the country, speak in raw terms of being dragged through the fires of hell. *BUT*—and this is a big, powerful transition point that makes all the difference when it comes to Gen-Z—they also write and speak about how they have traversed through the darkness and hellfire, how they have come out on the other side battered and torn and scarred, but victoriously intact, stronger, and enlightened. They—at ages seventeen, eighteen, and nineteen—embody a level of transformation, self-awareness, sensitivity, resilience, and maturity that has taken me more than four decades to achieve.

Reading essay after essay and hearing speech after speech, a stunning portrait of Gen-Z emerged early on for me: determined, tough, sentimental, optimistic, and compassionate survivors. From day one, I grinned ear to ear and my heart lit up in a million different directions, and it only grows brighter with every Gen-Z interaction I now continue to have.

Have I recognized this transitional journey from trauma to strength in the Gen-Zers I know? Have I personally experienced, or am I experiencing, a transitional journey from trauma to strength in my own life? If so, what can I learn from Gen-Zers to help me along the way?

ASK A GEN-ZER

What challenges have you faced in life and how have you overcome them, transitioning that challenge or trauma into strength?

CHAPTER 21

IT'S OK TO SEE THEM AS DIFFERENT.

THEY ARE!

Here's a new term for you: Generation Blindness.

We now live in a world where we often walk on eggshells around everyone, not wanting to offend someone by saying the wrong thing or acting inappropriately. Or, some head in the complete opposite, yet equally-as-blind, direction and say or do whatever they want—either purposely to be cruel or because they are ignorantly aloof with no concept of who they may be offending.

Blatant racism, misogyny, anti-LGBTQIA+ rhetoric, and other hateful discrimination aside, blinding ourselves to things like skin color or gender identification—out of fear or misinformed politeness—can also be offensive, and robs a person of crucial elements of their identity.

Gen-Z *is* different from the rest of us.

We're not their age. We don't have their lives in this moment in time. We don't see everything the same way as they might as young people. There are endless ways that we are different from them and they from us, and that's totally okay.

At one point, I discovered that as much as I cheerlead for Gen-Zers, I had a blind spot when it came to them. While travelling and sharing my adulation for Gen-Zers with older adults for whom this generation often remains both stereotype and enigma, I realized that I had to be more careful to not place them on pedestals like perfect, precious figurines in a curio cabinet to be *oohed* and *aahed* at. That would be unfair, and antithetical to who they are: authentically and unapologetically imperfect.

Instead of ignoring the differences or denying them—and thus succumbing to Generation Blindness—or, worst of all, judging them, ask Gen-Zers about those things that make them unique—as individuals and as a generation. Ask them why they think or act in certain ways. Ask them what their thoughts are on news, national and world affairs, and culture. Ask them what that tattoo or dyed hair means. Ask them what their gender identification means, if you don't understand it.

Ask. Ask. Ask. Then, listen, discuss, and find some mutual areas of agreement that can open everyone's eyes, but also don't be afraid of disagreeing with them. You'll find that Gen-Zers are great conversationalists once you engage them.

And please be willing to share the same from your perspective—what makes you different as an individual and as someone from your own unique generation.

To further explore the ways Gen-Zers are different, consider doing one of the activities or projects in the Activity Guide starting on page 205.

ASK YOURSELF

❝ When was the last time I recognized the ways I am different from the Gen-Zers in my life and had a discussion with them about that? When is the last time I asked Gen-Zers for their opinion about something?

ASK A GEN-ZER

❝ I noticed that your generation (or you) and my generation (or I) are so different when it comes to _____. Why do you think that is?

CHAPTER 22

THEY ARE
FORGIVING

One of the most difficult gifts to extend to others, and ourselves, is forgiveness, no matter how old we are. If forgiveness were an easy toss, then it would be worthless.

Gen-Zers come from a place of compassion and experience that is often founded on hard-earned wisdom beyond their years. So if you hurt or offend them, they will listen to and accept a sincere apology, which can sometimes be just as difficult to offer as it is to find the energy to accept. Sans an apology, they will still aspire to forgive because they recognize the redeeming power and freedom in that.

Even if the forgiveness needed is a long process (and it often is!), Gen-Zers will go along for that journey with you as long as you are authentic.

During an introductory presentation at the beginning of a school year, one of my students told our class that a few years earlier he had been the victim of a hit-and-run. While crossing the street with his sister to go to the park, a man driving a truck hit him and kept right on going. It was later discovered that the man drove to a gas station, scrubbed the blood off of his bumper, and simply went home.

My student further explained that he endured two life-threatening comas, but ultimately survived and is now thriving.

I knew he could handle this very big question, so I asked him, "Have you forgiven the man who hit you?"

"I'm working on it," he said. "And I know I'll eventually get there!"

I smiled. "I have no doubt you will!"

66 Do I have a hard time forgiving others? Why or why not?

66 Do you have a hard time forgiving others? Why or why not?

CHAPTER 23

THEY ARE
SURVIVORS

One of the most powerful and relatable threads I see woven from other generations straight through to Gen-Z is survival. Gen-Zers are survivors. Their battles are just different than ours.

The Greatest Generation fought and survived World War II. Baby Boomers fought and survived the Vietnam and Korean Wars. Gen-Xers fought and survived Operation Desert Storm. Millennials and other generations, including many Gen-Zers, have fought and survived domestic and international battles following the September 11, 2001, terrorist attack.

I often hear people of other generations, including some of my fellow Gen-Xers, say, "These young people today think they have it so tough! But they don't know what tough is—they never had to fight in a war!"

First off, I hope most Gen-Zers (and the rest of us!) never have to fight in a military-focused or any other war.

But, second, this doesn't mean they aren't fighting their own battles and wars right here on the home front.

One of the major battles for Gen-Z is mental health: confronting both their own issues head on and their unyielding commitment to being by the side of friends, family members, and others who are struggling and dying by suicide. Not to mention the ripples of other different challenges in all directions are many.

I've been blessed to work side by side with these Gen-Z survivors and have witnessed their struggles firsthand, like my student from the previous chapter who was plunged into two comas and a long recovery after a hit-and-run when he was a child. While in my class, he faced yet another huge challenge: he eventually dropped out of college because of the obligation he felt to get a full-time job to support his family, but he still remains laser-focused on his own future hopes and dreams.

Another Gen-Zer with whom I worked on a project is a survivor of one of the deadliest mass school shootings in US history. In high school now, she is a spectacular artist with the most beautiful spirit and boundless possibilities ahead of her.

I count both of these young people among the most brilliant, caring, and loving individuals—both survivors in every sense—I will ever know. They embody something I firmly believe in: From whom much is taken, much is also expected. *From whom much is taken, much is also expected.* When either of these young people walks into the room, their light is so bright!

Likewise, I have had countless talks with my students of color about racism. One particular common experience—what they call "The Look"—comes up again and again in our discussions. It's the obvious look, a glare really, that they often get when they are out in public, which is often fraught with suspicion, fear, sometimes outright hatred, and many times includes them being followed around stores and other places as if they are up to no good. All because of the color of their skin. This, too, is a battle that these particular Gen-Zers, and all people of color, confront every time they step out of their front door, or dorm room.

The very good news in all of this: Gen-Z has reconfirmed for me that survival and resilience come in many forms.

One time, I was a judge for a regional Poetry Out Loud competition where high school students were vying to go to the state finals.

A young woman stepped onto the stage in front of a packed auditorium, took a deep breath, and began performing the poem she had chosen. A few lines in, she stopped—clearly forgetting what came next. I mean, I had seen heart-wrenching moments like this in just about every teen-focused movie and TV show ever, but never in person from twenty feet away while sitting in the front row.

After a moment, the line came to her and she proceeded on. But soon, she hit a mind block again. She closed her eyes, clenched her fists, and took deep breaths. Meanwhile, my heart started pounding out of my chest, I broke into a sweat, I gripped the arms of my chair, and I held my breath! After what felt like an eternity, she began again, but then paused again, then began, and then paused. This went on until she had pushed through reciting the entire, very long poem.

Following the competition, I headed onstage to take a selfie with all of the Gen-Z contestants. But first, I sought out that young woman, who was holding back tears as her fellow students gathered around her in support.

"You may not have won," I told her, "but you literally had the most memorable and brilliant performance of the night!"

"Really?!" she said.

"OMG! The way you rallied and pushed through that poem, while taking all of us on a really heart-pounding journey with you—as in, *Will she remember the line or not? What's going to happen next?*—was the stuff of great movies and TV shows!" I told her. "It was both inspiring and so cinematic, even edge-of-your-seat entertaining—in that I-CAN'T-LOOK-BUT-I-CAN'T-STOP-LOOKING kind of way."

"Wow! I didn't think of it like that," she said, finally cracking a smile.

"You seriously have a talent, and an inner strength, that can't be learned; it's earned," I said. "And tonight you fantastically showcased just that, and inspired all of us!"

When we finally got around to taking the selfie, that young woman's smile was the biggest one in the group (next to mine)!

For sure, the wars, and other tragedies, of older generations have resulted in the loss of hundreds of thousands of lives and the post-traumatic effects on millions of others. But today, just among Gen-Z, mental health is a war impacting millions, with a suicide rate higher than any other generation in history—and this is all before you even factor in other challenges like the impact of school shootings, overdoses, bullying, racism, conflicts with family and friends, or anything else, including things like forgetting your memorized lines while standing alone on a stage in front of an auditorium full of people.

All this to say, someone from a previous generation, especially someone who saw war and tragedy up close, could have a very thoughtful, dynamic, and fruitful conversation with Gen-Zers, with both sides walking away more informed, inspired, and bolstered.

66 What are the wars and battles my generation has experienced? Has this helped me to better understand or relate to other generations and their challenges? Why or why not?

66 What are the biggest challenges and battles facing you and your generation?

CHAPTER 24

THE ONES WE
LOSE

By now, we all know someone who has attempted and/or died by suicide, or passed away because of an overdose, car accident, shooting, or some other tragic circumstance.

I come from a legacy of suicide—five suicides across three generations of my family—as well as having fellow Gen-Xers and other friends who have died by suicide.

Many of us know Gen-Zers specifically who fall into these categories, namely suicide. One of my students—one of the last young people I would have ever expected—died by suicide.

When tragedies like these strike, there are no words. And it's okay for there to be no words. It's okay for us to be at a loss for words or explanations, and to actually express that.

When my student died by suicide, I reached out to his cousin and best friend, who were also students of mine. I didn't say "I'm sorry," which is a throwaway phrase that always rings hollow to me and sounds like an uncomfortable filler for the fear or discomfort of saying anything else. What I did do was promise them that I would continue my advocacy for mental health on behalf of Gen-Z with even more vigor and dedication. That promise of positive action meant a lot to them, more than any words of sympathy I could have mustered.

On a warm summer day, I sat alone quietly in front of my student's grave, which is in a beautiful corner of a small rural cemetery. I studied the dates on the stone—2001–2020—and the various mementos that family and friends, and teammates, had left. I took particular notice of the small white moth that flew over, gently tapped me on the knee, and then flew off into the nearby trees. And I also made the same promise to this Gen-Zer—now frozen in time, eternally nineteen years old—as I did to his cousin and best friend, that his story wasn't going to end there. That was one way I could process his loss.

There will always be the ones we lose. It's what we choose to do then that makes all the difference.

66 How have I been affected by the loss of young people I know, especially from suicide? What actions did I take following those losses? What actions can I take in the future?

ASK A GEN-ZER

66 What is the best thing I can do for you to help you through this loss or challenge?

CHAPTER 25

THEY KNOW WHEN YOU'RE WASTING THEIR TIME BUT THEY'RE POLITE ENOUGH TO JUST IGNORE YOU

We all know when we are BSing someone—pontificating, making stuff up as we go, spoiling them, or simply lying.

Guess what? Gen-Zers have a keen sixth sense about this and can sniff out BS a mile away.

They value and respect straight talk, authenticity, and the truth, even when it's unpleasant to hear.

For instance, I watched one university's extreme virtue signaling over diversity, equity, and inclusion crash and burn particularly with the students of color on campus because they could see straight through the BS. I watched firsthand as the (now former) university president forcefully instituted virtue-signaling Band-Aid after virtual-signaling Band-Aid all over the campus—various race-related mandates, pontifications, and firings/hirings, but with no real strategy or true understanding of this critical issue or the campus community to back it up. I then also watched, with a smile, as the students—particularly the students of color—very publicly confronted her, demanding to know, "What is your actual strategy to help us?"

They called her out, and she had zero answers for them. Which is why she is now the former president of the school. Cue the huge applause for those students who called BS and demanded the respect and worth they deserve.

Sometimes, the BS we shovel out is with good intentions—to protect their feelings and lessen their burden. But still, if it walks like a duck and acts like a duck . . . A prop I would use here is any one of the countless, vapid one-sheeters and posters that older folks love to hang on school walls and community bulletin boards, declaring things like "10 Ways to Stress Less" or displaying some cliché quote we've all seen a million times super-imposed over an equally cliché stock photo of a calm stream or sunset. Cue the rolled eyes of every Gen-Z passerby (and me), if they even bother to look at it.

Even wrapped in a heart, BS is still just that.

Gen-Zers can handle the truth. They will often even help lead you to the solutions or the help that you or they may need with a particular situation, if they can see that you are coming from a sincere place of wanting to make a positive difference.

66 Do I ever BS the young people I know? If so, how and why?

66 Do you find that older adults BS you and your generation a lot? If so, in what ways? And if so, how does that make you feel?

CHAPTER 26

WHAT'S UP WITH NOT TURNING ON THE ZOOM CAMERAS?

I'll be the first to admit that the more insight and answers I gain to the question of "Who is Generation Z?" the more questions I have.

Such as, amidst the new Zoom World we live in: Why do the majority of Gen-Zers keep their cameras turned off during group meetings?

I have experienced this with my own students, as well as with Gen-Zers of all ages across the country whose classes and other groups I've Zoomed into for my various related projects.

This is another one of those battles I choose to pick sides wisely on, and I never make a fuss over having to address and constantly stare at blank squares with names on them for an hour straight. I understand that for some young people they may not feel like being on camera that day (or any day)—maybe because of social anxiety or other mental issues—and for others they are perhaps self-conscious about what's in the background inside their homes. Likewise, some have their cameras off because they are literally at work, multitasking, and indeed juggling, between the course they need to graduate and the job they need to pay for the course and to make a living.

What I have found to be less true (*Gee, surprise!*) is the stereotype that the cameras are off because the Gen-Zers aren't paying attention or aren't even there. Of course, I've caught a few in these disappearing acts, but they're the exception not the rule. When I purposely test this stereotype—especially because I like blasting through stereotypes as much as I enjoy obliterating stigmas—by randomly asking someone a question, the answer almost always comes, swiftly and sincerely, from behind that black square with the name on it.

However, on a humorous note: almost all the cameras do magically turn on when I suggest we take a group screenshot selfie! Or, when they want to introduce me to their dogs, cats, and once even a goat.

ASK YOURSELF

❝ During Zoom meetings, why do I choose to have my camera on or off? What should the etiquette be on this?

ASK A GEN-ZER

❝ When Zooming, do you have your camera on or off? Why? What do you think the etiquette on this should be?

112

CHAPTER 27

THEY JUST WANT
RESPECT
AND PEOPLE TO LISTEN TO THEM

Part of the joy I have as a teacher is getting to share my other career paths—as an author, artist, and advocate—with my students.

Any time I travel for whatever reason, I always ask whomever is organizing my trip to also find me a group of Gen-Zers and a group of mental health experts to visit with and learn from. And most of the time, somewhere along in these trips, I'm also talking, either formally or informally, to other generations about Gen-Z, all to help these young people to further introduce themselves to the world.

Before these trips, and even projects like this book, I always ask my students and other Gen-Zers around me: "What do you want me to tell the world about your generation?"

The replies are consistent: "We just want respect and people to listen to us."

66 Do I respect and *really* listen to the young people in my life? Why or why not? How can I respect and listen to young people even more attentively than I already do?

ASK A GEN-ZER

66 Do you feel that older generations respect and *really* listen to you and your generation? Why or why not?

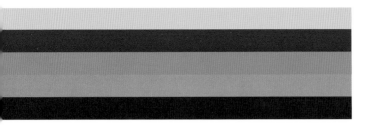

CHAPTER 28

BIG QUESTION:

IF GEN-ZERS ARE SO OPEN AND COURAGEOUS ABOUT THEIR MENTAL HEALTH STRUGGLES, THEN WHY DO THEY STILL HAVE

THE HIGHEST SUICIDE RATE OF ANY GENERATION IN HISTORY?

Let's start here: I don't know what I don't know. And I trust you don't either, correct?

For years, I touted Gen-Z's courage and honesty, and resilience, in sharing their mental health struggles to anyone who would listen. A lot of people did listen and did appreciate the more accurate portrait I painted beyond the stereotypes and stigmas they had previously been led to believe about these young people.

Then, one of my best friends—a fellow Gen-Xer—asked me: "If Gen-Zers are so open and courageous about their mental health struggles, *like you say they are*, then why do they still have the highest suicide rate of any generation in history?"

WOW! That question stopped me in my tracks. It's a great question.

Then it occurred to me: both of those points—facts, really—can be and are true.

They are open and courageous about their mental health struggles. YAY!!!

They do have the highest suicide rate of any generation in history. UGH!!!

I am now on an ongoing mission to unpack and answer this question. The answer is not simple. Even if I don't reach any definitive conclusions, I can at least get closer to an explanation.

But for now, I simply don't know what I don't know.

66 If Gen-Zers are so open and courageous about their mental health struggles, then why do I think they still have the highest suicide rate of any generation in history?

66 If Gen-Zers are so open and courageous about their mental health struggles, then why do you think your generation still has the highest suicide rate of any generation in history?

CHAPTER 29

IT'S ALWAYS THE ONES YOU

LEAST EXPECT

No doubt, many of you already know this by heart, likely a broken heart.

During our first class together, and later in our first one-on-one meeting in my office on campus, a student of mine, whom I previously mentioned in Chapter 24, told me all about his love of finance and Wall Street. He had even started investing in the stock market, and read every business book he could get his hands on. He also shared with me his vision for a long-term, well-planned future pathway to success and for living a happy life.

I was enormously impressed by his vision and determination, and relieved to think, *Oh, I don't have to worry about you!*

I told him, "Someday we'll all be working for you!"

He smiled ear to ear—a smile I was fortunate to see every week for several months.

A year later, at around 1:30 pm on a Saturday afternoon, he fatally shot himself. This was a day after he had spent one last time partying with his friends on a warm Friday night in rural Pennsylvania.

His best friend, who was also my student, sent me the last photograph taken of them together that night. I continue to carry that photo with me always.

This suicide only added more fuel to the question: If Gen-Zers are so open and courageous about their mental health struggles, *like I say they are*, then why do they still have the highest suicide rate of any generation in history?

One time, while meeting with me in my office, an Asian-American student—a brilliant pianist, whose playing I often heard gloriously echoing through the halls of our building—expressed that she was thinking of killing herself the following weekend while at home. Struggling with various issues, she also spoke to me about the heightened stigmas around mental health within her Asian family and culture. Thankfully, we were able to get her the counseling she needed, and the music went on.

Likewise, many of my African-American students have spoken to me about how mental health stigmas are even more pervasive in their communities than in the larger society. They also expressed how they are determined to use their own experiences and struggles to help turn that tide of understanding in a healthier and more positive direction.

Another student—athletic, intellectual, humorous, the picture of the American Dream in the making—whom I had in a few different courses I taught was diagnosed with four mental health disorders, diagnoses that shifted over time.

The first time I learned about this was when he asked me to step outside in the hall for a moment so he could talk to me.

"Do you mind if I skip class today?" he asked.

"Sure, no problem, but what's up?" I replied.

"I didn't sleep at all last night," he said. "I was up all night with panic attacks."

Having someone slam my head into the nearby block wall would have been less of a surprise. The picture of the American Dream in the making instantly got much more complicated.

I spent the following year watching him go from a healthy young guy to losing weight, growing pale, and struggling through adjustments to find the right medicine and to muster the energy to simply sit through class. Luckily, he has emerged healthy and happy on the other end.

Understanding that challenges—including the extreme of suicidal ideation—often also afflict the individuals we least expect is a valuable lesson in how we need to more mindfully view Gen-Zers, and others. This reminder also challenges our own invocation, even unknowingly, of stereotypes.

ASK YOURSELF

66 When have I encountered a tragedy or challenge involving a young person and thought, *They are the last person I would have expected to* _____?

ASK A GEN-ZER

66 Are you ever surprised to learn about tragedies or challenges that your friends or fellow Gen-Zers are going through, because you never expected that of them? Why or why not?

CHAPTER 30

THEY ARE WISE BEYOND THEIR YEARS, AND MAYBE EVEN BEYOND YOURS

You don't have to take my word for it here. I invite you to sit down with one or more of the Gen-Zers in your life, pick a topic—any topic (just don't be boring about it, since nobody likes boring)—and ask them what they think.

Recently, I arrived early at a restaurant where I was meeting friends for lunch. As I waited (I was really early, and the only diner there at the time), the Gen-Z waiter asked me from across the room, "So what do you think about the Middle East?"

I was like, "Huh? What part? Ummm, I don't know." He had stumped me for sure. But the randomness—to me at least—of such a question made me smile. *That's Gen-Z for you*, I chuckled to myself.

He then proceeded to give me a fascinating mini-lesson on Israel and Palestine, teaching me in about fifteen minutes what almost twenty combined years of my own education, and my avidly following current events, never did.

You may naturally wonder, *Where does this wisdom come from at such an early age?* I could throw out a few theories, such as the 24/7 nonstop news cycle across multiple media platforms including things like Twitter and TikTok, exposure to more diversity of individuals and content in schools and other settings, a larger focus on teaching critical thinking in schools, and so on. And the answer is definitely in there somewhere. But as I advised from the beginning of this book, if you want to know the most authentic answer to this question, find the nearest Gen-Zer and just ask them!

66 Do I know any Gen-Zers whom I would call "wise beyond their years"? Why or why not?

ASK A GEN-ZER

66 Do you think you are wise beyond your years? Why or why not?

CHAPTER 31

OLDER GENERATIONS, PLEASE TAKE NOTE:

JUST TALK TO THEM.

THEY WILL TALK BACK. YOU HAVE MORE IN COMMON THAN YOU THINK!

You'll hear me say this again and again: Please take the first step and talk to Gen-Zers, and they will respond.

I was once at a holiday party where the age range of the guests spanned teenagers to someone in their nineties. When a fifteen-year-old arrived with his family, he promptly sat in a corner and started reading one of the two books he had brought with him.

I watched with amusement the quizzical looks he got from the hosts and other guests. I mean, this was a party after all. I only smiled and was fascinated by what I was seeing. I certainly was not surprised or offended by his behavior at all.

When this Gen-Zer—whom I had never met before—got up and started to walk past me, I simply asked, "What are your books about?" He instantly lit up, told me the riveting premises of both books, and then for the next hour we engaged in a far-reaching conversation—covering high school athletics, video games, manga, mental health, how his high school is missing the mark big time when it comes to his generation, the state of the world, and the difference between being "influenced" versus being "inspired" when it comes to the media's negative impact on young people.

This Gen-Zer could seriously teach a college seminar course! Yet it would have been way too easy for us older adults to ignore him as he read alone in the corner and simply label him as rude, weird, or you name it. Which I suspect some others at the party did do. Meanwhile, I was in awe, since he reconfirmed so much of why I respect and admire his generation.

So, now let's restart this little discussion here from a point of contention between *all* generations. All older generations do this to the new kids on the block: they see the younger generations in varying shades—depending on whom you're talking to—of radical, lazy, rude, uninformed, naïve, consumed with the latest technology, they listen to awful music, they run wild . . .

You get the picture here. In fact, your generation was no doubt once (or still is) labeled in similar terms by those older than you. And, come to think of it, we're even labeled by those younger than us as well—"OK, Boomer!" One Gen-Zer also once told me that she even has a fear of older people, which it turns out is actually a real, albeit thankfully rare, thing: gerontophobia.

I'm sure Gen-Zers will have a few things to say about Generation Alpha—whom I'm already celebrating in a brighter light as The Imagination Generation (those born during or after 2013)—that may not be exactly on the mark. In fact, that's already happening.

Some Gen-Zers I've talked to have complained about how their little Gen-Alpha brothers and sisters are so attached to their iPads, cell phones, and other technology that they're practically cyborgs. One Gen-Zer said that his little brother even starts punching him if he tries to take away his iPad! And another's Gen-Alpha sister screams and bites to defend her nonstop screen time! However, I'm hopeful that this unprecedented access to technology and other resources from birth onward will allow kids today to utilize their imaginations unlike any other generation before them. For sure though, Gen-Alphas, no more punching, screaming, or biting, please. That's definitely not a good look, and it's the recipe for some very unwanted stereotypes right off the bat.

I wrote a memoir—*Five Years in Heaven: The Unlikely Friendship That Answered Life's Greatest Questions*—about the power and benefits of cross-generational relationships and the sharing of fun and wisdom that takes place. In my case, this was a life-changing friendship started when I was thirty-one with an eighty-seven-year-old nun and artist who ran the ceramic shop at our local convent.

And this book you're holding in your hands right now is very much a tribute to the power and impact of cross-generational relationships—namely that this Gen-Xer has cultivated with Gen-Zers across the country and beyond.

I would love to eavesdrop on a discussion between veterans who fought and survived wars and Gen-Zers who are battling and surviving mental health and other challenges. Or Baby Boomers chatting with Gen-Zers about the threads of similarity and difference they all share, especially via pop culture and the young-at-heart vibe for adventure. Or Gen-Xers and Gen-Zers comparing and contrasting growing up in the 1980s versus today. After all, every generation can relate to discovering and realizing how "each one of us is a brain, and an athlete, and a basket case, a princess, and a criminal," and so much more!

In fact, we are all here, on these pages, because we already have cross-generational relationships with Gen-Zers and are working to expand and elevate those to even greater heights of understanding and productivity.

Point being: You have more in common with Gen-Zers than you think, so have fun discovering what that is. For starters, join them in creating and playing the Name That Generation Game on page 229, or option number three for either the Pick A Word, Any Word activity on page 219 or Pick A Topic, Any Topic activity on page 221.

66 **What do I have in common with other generations, especially Gen-Z?**

66 **What do you think you have in common with other generations?**

130

CHAPTER 32

STUDY

BRAIN ANATOMY

Don't let this one scare you, even though it sounds *really* scary!

Trust me, had I majored in psychology, psychiatry, or anatomy, I would have failed out. Maybe traditional school pedagogies aren't a fit for me either and/or my brain just doesn't work in the way one needs it to in order to pursue those fields professionally.

However, because of my ever-growing curiosity and advocacy around mental health, I want to continue learning about things like anxiety, depression, suicide, and trauma, and how everything impacts and filters through the brain.

I do this by taking every chance I get to listen to those going through mental health struggles, those who have survived suicide attempts, and experts in all fields related to mental health and the brain. I always have them speak to me in simple terms that I'll understand and remember. I never take notes, because then I'm not really listening. I pay attention, and I consider it a success if I walk away with one or two new facts, or stories, that I know I'll remember.

What I won't remember: limbic, diencephalon, or medulla oblongata. (I can't even remember the name of the medication I take for my own journey with anxiety: Citalopram.) All are important for sure, but all are way above my pay grade as far as memorizing goes.

What I will remember: That everything we experience, including trauma, has to go through our fight-or-flight, reptilian brainstem first before it reaches the top, rationally-thinking and contemplating layers of our uniquely human brain. And that when we are talking to another person, we are first speaking to their brainstem—*if* our message and how we are communicating it makes it past their brainstem, then and only then will it proceed to the upper levels of their brain.

The one big, fancy word I have committed to memory, because it's my all-time favorite fact about the brain, is *neuroplasticity*. This is the brain's proven ability to rewire itself—positively or negatively—based on our experiences throughout our lives. For a more detailed, jargon-laced definition of the word, look it up. (It's always good to have at least one fancy word to pull out of your back pocket if needed, and especially if it's one that really interests you.)

Likewise, I always invite mental health experts to speak with my students and other Gen-Zers with whom I cross paths, especially since I know mental wellness and advocacy are so important to them. My only two requests to these experts for their presentations are that: one, they use simple words and concepts that everyone can remember, and, two, that they also use simple terminology to explain the all-important concept of how past traumas can continue to catch up to us throughout our lives—via PTSD and everyday minor-to-major triggers—starting with our brains where they are stored.

Speaking of which, my newest acquisition is a medical school–grade model of the human brain that sits on my desk at home. I may not remember everything about the brain, but I'm sure enjoying the journey of learning, healing, and fun that I'm having because of it.

All of this takes on even greater significance considering our mission here when you keep in mind (literally!) that the current brains of Gen-Zers are still growing and developing! And on that note, I suggest you check out The Gen-Z Brain Project activity on page 223.

ASK YOURSELF

66 What do I really know about the human brain? In what ways can I learn more about the brain? How often do I think about my brain?

ASK A GEN-ZER

66 What do you know about the human brain? How often do you think about your brain?

CHAPTER 33

THE 20TH CENTURY IS
ANCIENT HISTORY
TO THEM

Before I go any further here, I highly suggest that you first eradicate the phrase "That makes me feel so old!" from your vocabulary. That mindset isn't helping anyone, especially you!

Now, as to the fact that the twentieth century is akin to ancient history for Gen-Zers, I'm sure many of you have already discovered this, and, if not, I'll prepare you for the shock. To Gen-Zers, who at the most were three years old at the turn of the century—meaning 1999 to 2000—the twentieth century is, indeed, ancient history—a time before their time.

Remember how we thought about the year 1900, let alone the 1800s, when we were growing up? Well, the 1900s are Gen-Z's equivalent of the 1800s for us.

Princess Diana, Columbine, the original *Beverly Hills, 90210*, the original *Saved by the Bell*, Duran Duran, Madonna, Depeche Mode, Elvis, Ronald Reagan, JFK, The Great Depression, the World Wars . . . all ancient history to them. At most, some of them were only four years old on September 11, 2001.

Just remember that when you're talking to them. I don't want you to be caught off guard if they don't know what floppy disks, Walkman, legwarmer, disco, or Roaring (19)20s mean. For further insight, I suggest playing a few rounds of the Name That Generation Game on page 229.

That said, it makes this Gen-Xer very proud to hear many Gen-Zers express their affection specifically for our coming-of-age 1980s. More than a few have told me, "I wish I had grown up in the eighties; it was such a better and easier time!" (See, Gen-Z has some positive, albeit not completely accurate, stereotypes about us Gen-Xers, too!)

When I hear this, I just smile and nod, hearing Simple Minds' "Don't You Forget About Me" blasting in my head, and agreeing to a point. It was a great era, certainly not perfect. But I don't want to burst their big-hair, neon-is-the-attitude, *Breakfast Club*–infused bubble too quickly (we usually get to that reality when I have to explain why some of their parents and others my age seem close-minded, judgmental, and so on to them—as in, despite some totally rad fashions and music, we also dealt with more than our fair share of trauma and challenges when we were their age.)

66 How often do I say, "That makes me feel so old!"?

66 When you hear twentieth century or 1900s, what comes to mind?

CHAPTER 34

THEIR FAITH AND SPIRITUALITY

ARE THERE—IT'S JUST NOT ALWAYS

OBVIOUS

When I'm talking to older adults about Gen-Zers, a question I almost always get is: "Are they religious?"

As with any generation, or any one person, the answer to that question is way more layered than a simple yes or no. (And, again, if you want to know, you can always just ask them.)

But this is what I do know: for starters, Gen-Zers are really good and compassionate and caring people.

As for specific faith preferences, there are those who speak openly and enthusiastically about their faith and those who say nothing. Just like other folks on planet Earth.

But here's a clue to the answer: one semester I passed around two blank sketchbooks in my classes (see activity on page 209) and told them I'd hand them out at the beginning of every class meeting during the following four months and that the only rule was that nothing was off limits as to what they could express inside the books. They'd have complete freedom to write, draw, scribble, tape, or glue whatever they wanted on those blank pages.

At the end of the semester, the sketchbooks were packed. But one of the consistent entries throughout was Bible passages in different handwriting—and not only short scriptures, but long ones that had clearly been committed to memory. (And, *of course*, there was also the sketch of a penis that another student later modestly covered with masking tape, which made me chuckle and reminded me that while wise beyond their years, these students were still teens prone to mischief.)

ASK YOURSELF

66 **What assumptions do I have about the faith or spirituality of Gen-Zers?**

ASK A GEN-ZER

66 **What religious or faith-based beliefs and practices do you have?**

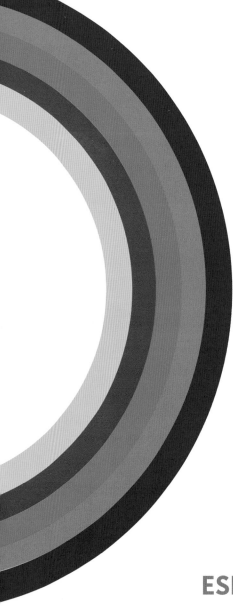

CHAPTER 35

THEY LIKE TO CLIMB ON FURNITURE

AND EVEN RESCUE TRUCKS,

ESPECIALLY FOR SELFIES

One of my favorite attributes about Gen-Z is while polite to a fault, if coaxed, they are always game for a little innocent mischief and fun, which is very reminiscent of us Gen-Xers (though I don't think we have ever needed much coaxing on things like this). This is especially true when a selfie is involved.

As an artist, the visual of any situation—and selfies are definitely a situation—is super important to me. Often, this includes seeing what I can get away with and who I can bring along for the fun ride.

Case in point: In the past, when I have climbed on top of furniture at the university—couches, desks, podiums, tables in the library—or once a rescue vehicle at our local Elkland Search and Rescue headquarters after I did a presentation there, and I told the nearby Gen-Zers to join me for a photo, two things happened . . .

First, they looked around at other so-called authority figures (until I snapped their attention back to me) and then they politely asked me, "Are we allowed to do that?"

To which this Gen-Xer replied, "By the time anyone yells at us, it'll be too late: we'll have had our fun and gotten our selfie!"

With that, the second thing happened: they all immediately raced to the top with me and struck a smiling pose!

All this to say, Gen-Zers like to have fun just like the rest of us, but as with starting conversations with them, sometimes you have to be the lead instigator of fun and mischief. Which is fine with me!

" Am I a total rule follower, or am I open to a little innocent mischief and fun from time to time?

" Are you a rule follower, or are you open to a little innocent mischief and fun from time to time?

CHAPTER 36

THEY ARE STILL WONDERFULLY PRONE TO MISCHIEF

Not to be confused with the previous chapter wherein we older adults play instigator, there are also a lot of Gen-Zers who don't need much, or any, coaxing when it comes to their own mischievous vibe.

While I love how wise and progressive beyond their years Gen-Zers are, I'm equally thrilled to be reminded that they are still prone to creating mischief all on their own.

With everything impacting them—mental health, competitive academics, sports, extracurricular activities, jobs, the ups and downs of personal relationships, social media, and national and global issues like racism, gender inequality, and climate change—they are still youths. And they deserve the opportunity like we all had for some playful chaos, making some mistakes, and acting their age.

To glowingly illustrate my point here, picture this scene: a high school installation of my eighteen-foot-long, Participatory Art mural titled *THE SMILE THAT CHANGED THE WORLD (is yours)*, for which participants were invited to paint smiles and other details on dozens of blank faces. Hundreds of Gen-Zers with paintbrushes in hand came and went in front of the very long canvas—total joy, but also total and fun chaos.

Over the course of the six-hour installation, one particular Gen-Zer kept eluding us as he or she drew a cigarette (or something else!) coming out of one face's very happy smile.

School officials would quietly ask other students to paint over the cigarette by making the smile bigger. But minutes later, the cigarette—even larger—would reappear. This happened about four times before a school official finally stood guard by this one face on the mural, which now had a really, really huge smile on it. The elusive Gen-Z culprit here—who clearly has a great sense of humor, and mischief—was never caught, which, while I certainly don't like smoking, still makes me laugh to this day.

I would love to engage him or her in a discussion about everything, starting with: How did you manage to get away with that in front of literally hundreds of people?

66 What is my reaction to the mischief caused by Gen-Zers? And why?

66 Do you think you, or your generation, are mischievous? Why or why not? If so, is that a good or bad thing? Please explain.

CHAPTER 37

THEY STAY UP ALL NIGHT, WHETHER YOU LIKE IT OR NOT.

SO HOW ABOUT A 2:00 AM CLASS?

One day, a student said to me, "I'm so sorry I missed your class—I over-slept."

I was like, "But our class is at 1:00 IN THE AFTERNOON!"

That's the moment I learned that many, if not most, Gen-Zers are up all night long. But be careful here, because it's easy for us to slip into a stereotype about the why.

Sure, for some, staying up late at times simply means hanging out with friends and goofing off. And then barely being able to keep their eyes open the next day.

For many others though, staying up all night can mean things like finishing homework and studying for tests; working the night shift; being on call for friends who may be going through a rough patch; going through their own insomnia-inducing anxiety, depression, or panic attacks; or playing video games as practice for competitions (which they've given me a whole new respect for—see Chapter 43).

Rather than criticize or judge them for their reasons or prowess as night owls, I instead posed the question: "What if schools, especially colleges and universities, offered courses at like 2:00 am?"

I felt like this fell nicely in line with my motto of meeting Gen-Zers where (and when) they are and helping them to rise from there.

The students loved the idea.

The schools and colleagues I've posed this suggestion to have yet to return my call. Yet they'll happily drag themselves and these young people out of bed for an 8:00 am class (now that craziness really does deserve a "NOT OK, Boomer!")!

66 What do I think of young people staying up all night, even if they are being productive?

66 Do you go to bed early or late, and why?

CHAPTER 38

THEY ARE WATCHING US, ESPECIALLY ON SOCIAL MEDIA—SO BE A ROLE MODEL

Gen-Zers are very astute observers. They are always watching us—how we act *and* react, what we say *and* what we don't say, and even what we post online.

By the time I walk into the first day of classes, my students already know more about me than I remember about myself. I know this because they'll refer to images on my social media pages, they'll ask me specific questions about the books I've written or art I've created or places I've traveled, they've watched clips of interviews I've done, and they'll quote from my website. This never ceases to amaze and amuse me. Many of them would make great investigators, and some are, indeed, pursuing careers in criminal justice.

This has become a powerful Note to Self for me: whenever I am posting something online, I'm aware that many Gen-Zers who follow me will see it. What exactly does this mean about my posts? For me, it doesn't change much about what I would normally post. But the fact that I like to post images and messages about having fun; living life to the fullest; my love of road trips to haunted places, climbing trees and other structures, and rescue dogs; and my advocacy on behalf of mental health, Gen-Z, and other issues takes on a whole new meaning and mission.

Likewise, when I'm conceptualizing new book and art projects, or accepting invitations to do this or that, or even deciding which boards—corporate or nonprofit—to serve on, I'm now always conscious of the young and impressionable eyes I have on me and how my actions and decisions will hopefully positively influence them.

" Am I a role model for young people? Why or why not?

" Who are your role models, and why?

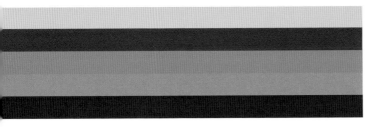

CHAPTER 39

WHAT WOULD
GEN-Z DO?

Remember the "WWJD" ("What would Jesus do?") motto trend? It was everywhere, and ultimately a positive message for many to live by.

Because of my respect and admiration for Gen-Z, across so many areas, I often now ask myself "What would Gen-Z do?" in the various situations I encounter.

For example, over the years, I have served on several non-profit and corporate board of directors. These experiences are always humbling honors for me, and great opportunities to both share my own skills and learn about new subjects. And to practice patience!

As I'm sure you well know from your own experiences, working with groups of people can be very challenging. In fact, when my students grumble any time I assign a group project, I tell them that while I totally get it, the dynamic of group projects—as in some members are control freaks and want to do everything, others are slackers and want to do virtually nothing, and still others vacillate in the middle somewhere—is something they will encounter throughout their lives. That never helps my case as the teacher assigning a group project, but there's a truth in there all the same that is worth understanding.

Many times, I found that the ideas and skills I was literally bringing to the table were downplayed, patronized, or even ignored amongst various fellow board members, which only caused my annoyance and frustration to fester.

Then, I implemented a new tactic for navigating the unique stew of personalities, ideas, and agendas that boards tend to embody. I started asking myself, *What would the Gen-Zers I know do in this situation?*

I didn't have to contemplate that for long. I knew they would lead compassionately, yet firmly, letting their voice and worth be heard loudly and clearly. And that's what I started to do, and that's when many of the challenging situations I encountered in the boardroom and beyond, and my own self-confidence, started to go in a much more positive and productive direction.

Especially as an educator and advocate, I want to be a role model. I want Gen-Zers to be proud of the work I'm doing, especially the work on their behalf. Sometimes, this begins with my respect and admiration of them being role models, and teachers, for me.

The next time you have a decision—great or small—to make or are in a challenging situation, asking yourself "What would Gen-Z do?" may yield some very interesting perspectives and outcomes for you as well.

" What positively influences me when I'm making a decision or doing something? Am I ever inspired in my own decision-making by what I've seen Gen-Zers do?

ASK A GEN-ZER

" What or who positively influences the way you make decisions?

CHAPTER 40

SOME
OF THEM
STILL USE

PAPER CALENDARS

In the spirit of making those of you who "feel old" feel a little better when you see youthful Gen-Zers, keep these two things in mind:

1. They don't see you as an age, only as someone who is either interesting, kind, and fun *or* annoying, judgmental, and to be politely avoided at all costs. (Just like I do.)

2. Many Gen-Zers still use paper calendars, as in writing with a pen or pencil on a paper calendar! (Just like I do.)

> **What things do I do that "feel old" to me, and why?**

> **Is there anything that makes you "feel old"?**

CHAPTER 41

RESEARCH: THEY HAVE EIGHT-SECOND ATTENTION SPANS. UMMM, ONLY IF YOU DON'T GIVE THEM SOMETHING INTERESTING TO ACTUALLY

PAY ATTENTION TO!

Occasionally, I'll peruse the studies and research being done on Gen-Z. At some point or another, every generation becomes lab rats.

Studies showing that Gen-Z's attention span is only like eight or so seconds particularly caught my eye. I'll refrain from criticizing this claim, because I think research of all kinds is important and that the ultimate truth is always more layered than a single number or label. However, this particular finding's unfortunate side effect of fueling stereotypes and stigmas is disheartening.

I know that my attention span is probably eight seconds or less, too, if I'm bored or feel left out.

For sure, I've seen Gen-Zers lose interest in something at lightning speed, but I also saw the boring material that was being presented or served up to them. I lost interest right along with them.

The lesson here for the rest of us: provide something interesting and relevant to them, teach them skills they can actually use and apply, and do it all respectfully—meaning, know your audience and don't waste their time—and I guarantee you'll extend that eight seconds into something productive and meaningful.

And on that note, I'll refer you to the Activity Guide starting on page 205, which will give you a few tricks up your sleeve for engaging and entertaining your Gen-Zers. The activities and projects can be easily adapted to fit the work you are doing with them.

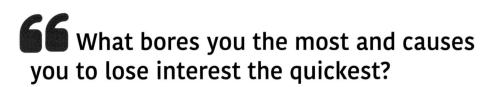 When working with Gen-Zers, am I boring them, even if I think the content I'm sharing is the most exciting thing on planet Earth? How can I better engage with Gen-Zers and hold their interest longer?

What bores you the most and causes you to lose interest the quickest?

CHAPTER 42

THIS APPROACH WILL FAIL EVERY TIME:

HARASSING THEM,

CANCELING THEM,

AND/OR GIVING THEM LOWER GRADES BECAUSE THEY DISAGREE WITH YOU ON POLITICS AND OTHER ISSUES

For everyone out there who does this, I know who you are! Gen-Zers have told me all about you, from coast to coast.

So heed my plea: let Gen-Zers have their own opinions, even if they vastly contradict your own. Instead of being triggered, becoming enraged, or secretly seething, and then belittling them in front of others, and then giving them lower grades or other punishments for having their own minds, please engage them in discussions and healthy debate.

Together with an entire campus of Gen-Zers, I myself experienced a dose of this rancid dynamic. A few years ago, I created a Participatory Art project titled *My America Is . . .* to be installed at a university. The piece consisted of a 9' x 6' wooden mural—which I had a fellow artist paint white with a black outline of the United States—that was then cut into three 3' x 6' pieces. The plan was for the three panels to travel around to different locations on the campus—the library, student center, sports center, and academic buildings—for two months during which time students, and anyone else, could write or draw their responses to the title prompt directly on the boards.

The goal of the project—which was sponsored by an academic program on campus—was to give participants the opportunity to share a piece of themselves and their unique American story through words and images, which would then collectively form a larger, diverse portrait of our America—all to facilitate a better understanding for all of us. I even personally met with the university president to secure her sign-off and to be assured that specifically the Gen-Zers on campus would be left to freely express their opinions, no matter what they were. She said yes, the project had her full support.

At the beginning of the live installation, I had the honor of visiting the panels with groups of Gen-Zers, watching them add their words and phrases and other images to the panels, and discussing them. However, within less than a week of the installation going live, the university abruptly removed all three panels from public view and participation. It was shut down.

I'll refrain from using the B(anned) word—though as an artist, being considered controversial and then essentially banned, I felt I had earned a certain new street cred. Which was a sentiment that the hip Gen-Zers on campus actually did express to me, to make me feel better (and it did!).

It was unfortunate to see this space where debate and conversations were happening, per my original mission, be silenced.

On those boards, difficult and inflammatory language dialogued alongside inspiring, insightful, and hopeful messages: *My America Is . . .* "Still learning, still growing," "divided," "resilient," "troubled," "Full of opportunities," "hurting," "In need of Jesus," "not free," "Taken for granted," "adventurous," "Doesn't like black people," "passionate," "Does not belong to me," "innovative," "In the hands of its people," "uneducated," "Systemic oppression," "A self-made nation," "stressed," "Scared of black power," "A community that has welcomed me—an immigrant," "joyful," "nuts," "A work in progress," "diverse," "Full of hope," "A place that I love," and "If America truly hated you, you wouldn't see this."

I was disappointed that *My America Is . . .* would never have the chance to serve its original purpose of offering Gen-Zers, and others, the freedom to engage in open and productive exchanges, and that my full vision would never be realized. Eventually,

I planned to have the completed large mural cut into small 2" x 2" pieces that would then become a new Participatory Art piece titled *Our America*. Passersby would be encouraged to take a piece of *Our America* home with them.

Two quickly-organized town halls were held on campus to discuss the project's removal. I attended both, sitting quietly in the back of the room. I was there to support the students and to have their backs. I was so proud to hear the Gen-Zers calmly, strategically, and brilliantly defend *My America Is . . .* and the need for a space where all viewpoints can be expressed, examined, and discussed—letting me know that my original mission had, indeed, progressed, thanks to them.

My eyes especially welled up as one young African-American student delivered an impassioned defense of the project, ending her remarks by saying, "This is the first time I have actually felt heard on this campus."

Meanwhile, I was amused by how awestruck and speechless many of the attending professors and the administrators, who had shut down the project, were as they listened to these incredible and sincere students. Again, mission completed—I realized that in a roundabout way I had helped the Gen-Zers on campus to further introduce themselves to the larger university community.

Gen-Z triumphed here. Those who shut down the installation did not.

Bottom line: Gen-Zers welcome healthy debate and thrive in that space. In fact, they can civilly and productively discuss partisan politics and social issues better than anyone, if given the chance.

But humiliating them, silencing them, canceling opportunities for them to express and create, and/or putting your stress, problems, and the mantle of world's weight on their shoulders is a lose-lose for all involved.

168

66 Do I ever negatively treat or interact with young people because they disagree with me about politics or other issues? How can I engage in more balanced and healthier discussions and debates with Gen-Zers, even when we disagree?

ASK A GEN-ZER

66 Have you ever been negatively treated or impacted because an older adult disagreed with your opinions about politics or other issues?

CHAPTER 43

VIDEO GAMERS MAY RULE THE WORLD SOON, AND
THAT'S OK!

While I only talk old-school Atari—Pong, anyone?—Gen-Zers have elevated gaming to a whole new level of fun, competition, and professional possibilities.

Before we proceed any further here, consider this: the US military and corporations are actively recruiting video gamers as the next generation of soldiers and corporate leaders.

Talk about stereotypes! Who doesn't conjure the image of strung-out, violence-prone teens lounging in a dark basement somewhere playing video games 24/7? This stereotype is as old as Pac-Man himself. And while some gamers—from several different generations—may literally still breathe continued life and confirmation into this stereotype, making it at least semi-true, Gen-Zers aren't resting on those tired, old laurels.

Gaming has gone international and is a bona fide competitive sport, featuring sponsorships and lucrative prizes. For military and corporate recruiters, in most of these gamer-athletes they see honed instincts, the art of strategy, quick reaction time, proficient group work, innovative creativity, and out-of-the-box thinking. Not to mention, some very interesting personalities.

Not a gamer myself, and even a little skeptical at first years ago, Gen-Zers have taught me that gaming is more than a fun pastime, and that it can be more akin to the most important classroom or training ground on planet Earth, or whatever world they're inhabiting onscreen at any given moment of competition.

66 **What do I really think about young gamers? Do I see any benefits for Gen-Zers who are avid gamers?**

66 **Are you a gamer? If so, are you in competitions? What skills do you need to be a gamer, and/or what skills do you learn as a gamer? Tell me about why you're a gamer and what you hope to do with those skills.**

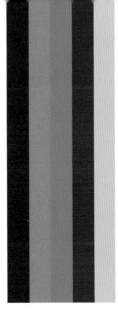

CHAPTER 44

THEY ARE STUDYING, AND WE ARE PREPARING THEM, FOR JOBS THAT MAY NOT EVEN EXIST YET (AND, BTW, UNDECLARED MAJORS ARE AWESOME!)

The world is moving super fast. Creation, invention, and innovation are happening quicker than ever before.

Which means in two years, three years, four years, maybe even next week, new jobs and opportunities will emerge that most of us can't even dream about at this moment. Keep in mind, the first Gen-Zer went into space at age eighteen, which wouldn't have been possible even just a few months before that actually happened.

For those of us who work with Gen-Zers, it's our job to prepare them for those future jobs and opportunities, and even communicate this exciting dynamic of infinite possibilities to them to begin with. But how do we prepare them for something we can't even see or fathom yet?

We can start by simply reading the room.

College isn't for all of them, and that's okay. Gen-Z is proving there are other pathways. Skills-based and corporate training programs, and YouTube, and even gap years spent exploring are quickly answering this need.

They want skills to take with them anywhere. Hands-on skills like how to build this and how to create that, and the critical skills to think about everything.

They will also job hop—we know this—so we need to prepare them and plan for that.

Call it humility, or I prefer to blame it on restrictive résumé templates and advisors who have no clue of what makes this generation tick, but Gen-Zers are notorious for selling themselves short on résumés and rarely does anyone call them out on it. But I do! To me, crafting a résumé is like assembling a fun, colorful, and fascinating puzzle.

If you are working on résumés with Gen-Zers, peel back their humility and polite uncertainty, and ask them to brainstorm everything they have done and all the skills they have, no matter how far-fetched some things may seem. From that master list, help them to curate a résumé (including creating new categories, such as Multilingual Experience, Gaming Experience & Awards, Performance & Presentation Experience, Technology Repair Experience, Skills-Based Experience, Published Works, and Customer Service Experience) that sets them apart and answers the needs of today's well-rounded workforce, not that of forty—or even ten—years ago.

And, by the way, it's okay if their résumé goes over one page. I find it humorous that any Gen-Z résumé over one page tends to trigger academics and send them into fits of ridiculousness. Hello, have you actually met these young people and heard of everything they have packed into only a few decades or less of living and working?

If Page One of a résumé is interesting, a prospective employer will certainly take the time to flip to Page Two. And if said prospective employer is not willing to flip to Page Two of a really compelling résumé, then I would highly recommend that the Gen-Zer not work there, because they won't be fully appreciated.

Finally, believe the stereotypes or not (I'd highly suggest that you please don't), Gen-Zers actually do understand the value of money. They know when their money is well spent and when it is being wasted, especially on an education that is giving them nothing in return. They value quality, so it's up to us to provide that opportunity for them—meeting them where they are and helping them to rise from there.

And, PS: starting off college as an undeclared major is an awesome thing, especially if a student isn't sure what they want to do. For some reason, the "undeclared major" has fallen victim to both stereotype and meme, but these students deserve the respect and room to explore. Not to mention, they are often among the most brilliant students in the classroom.

" Am I preparing the Gen-Zers in my life for jobs that may not even exist yet? If so, how? If not, how can I do so?

" Do you feel prepared for future jobs that may not even exist yet?

CHAPTER 45

THEY ARE GREAT LISTENERS, AND APPRECIATE WHEN YOU ARE

HONEST

AND
VULNERABLE

WITH THEM

Many older generations tend to think that young people run their mouths and claim to know everything. And, guess what: vice versa.

By now, you know this stereotype is just that, for any generation—though we all know individuals of all ages who love to hear themselves *blah blah blah* on and on, and who really do think they know everything or, at the very least, they have an opinion on literally everything.

There is an art to listening. It's a gift to be a good listener. Gen-Zers are good listeners.

Letting them hear what you have to say or confiding in them—like your own struggles with mental health or other challenges, or your joys and successes—helps them relate to you and know that you understand them and what they are going through along their own life journeys of ups and downs.

66 Am I a good listener, especially with young people? Why or why not? If not, how can I become a better listener?

ASK A GEN-ZER

66 Do you think you're a good listener? Why or why not? If not, how can you become a better listener?

CHAPTER 46

THEY THINK NOBODY LIKES THEM, AND LOVE TO HEAR THAT

PEOPLE DO

Every time I meet a Gen-Zer or group of them, I tell them that I am a #1 fan of their generation.

Almost to a person, they always get a surprised look on their face and say, "Really?! I thought everybody hated us."

I'm going to just leave you with that, to ponder.

66 Was I aware that many Gen-Zers think older adults don't like them? Why or why not? What can I do to change this?

66 Do you think most older adults dislike your generation? Why or why not?

CHAPTER 47

THE BLESSING
AND CURSE
OF SOCIAL MEDIA

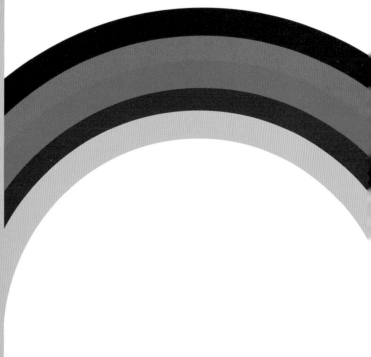

You've heard it; you've maybe even barked it yourself: "Social media is the problem! That's why these kids are insecure, are obsessed with how they look, get bullied, can't focus, and are killing themselves!"

If that's you talking, then please take a deep breath!

Like anything else, it's definitely not that simple. A good place to start decoding the mystery and stereotype of social media is to ask Gen-Zers what they think of it and how they use it. Don't assume, when you can go straight to the source for the answer.

Combined with any preconceived notions you may already have on the topic, you'll definitely hear enough from Gen-Zers to fuel your dark cloud of Social Media = Evil, Bad, Downfall of Society.

However, you will also hear how social media is one reason why Gen-Zers have learned to be confident and comfortable in speaking their truths aloud. Because via social media they have discovered other Gen-Zers just like them—whatever "just like them" happens to be—across the country and the world. Social media has become a place of community and belonging for them, in a way that no other previous generation has experienced.

But a word of advice: don't follow the Gen-Zers you know on social media if your intention is to police them and spy on their every move. First off, they are on to that big time. And, second, they have their ways to get around your prying eyes (see Chapter 9), even if your intentions are more in the name of love and concern than simply being nosy. You will never beat them at this game!

66 What do I think the impact of social media is on young people?

66 What does social media mean or represent to you and your generation?

CHAPTER 48

THEY ARE MARVELOUSLY

SENTIMENTAL

Being sentimental is an easy trait to spot in Gen-Zers. This is probably something you already know, but it's so genuine and endearing with them that it bears repeating and highlighting.

One only has to look at the people, places, activities, and things that Gen-Zers hold dear to their hearts to see their sentimental side shine.

Two of my students proudly showed me a dog tag and a compass—both on chains—that their brothers gave them and which they always wear. Another Gen-Zer showed me her deceased grandma's scripted signature tattooed on her arm, which had been copied from a card her grandma had once sent to her. While meeting on Zoom, one student pointed out *The Breakfast Club* movie poster hanging behind him next to framed posters of all the high school musicals that he had performed in. And next to his laptop, on his desk, was a photo of himself with his best friend who died by suicide.

Among other revealing insights, *The Gen-Z Time Capsule* that I created in collaboration with The Andy Warhol Museum has proven to be a treasure trove of sentimental clues to this generation. There are pictures with family and friends and beloved pets, a heart-shaped hole in a leaf with the sun shining through, a jar of porcupine quills that had been a gift from a deceased grandpa, a saved Pog set from a mother, trophies and medals from years of wrestling, and so much more.

During the national launch event at a high school in Maryland for The Kindness Rocks & Smiles Community Project™ that I co-founded with The Kindness Rocks Project founder Megan Murphy, when the media showed up I instantly went into Gen-Z Publicist mode. It was important for me to make sure that these young people got to share their thoughts with the larger community, who would be tuning into the nightly news later that evening. And they didn't disappoint as I directed them to step in front of the camera.

Off the cuff, and without missing a beat, one young man said, "Nowadays, everyone has become so distant and they compare themselves to other people, and that really damages the mind . . ." He went on to explain the importance of implementing projects and actions that will "warm up hearts." A young woman spoke of how "kindness really holds people together." And another young woman emphatically stated, "It's very important for us to still be kind to each other and come together to support one another through whatever we need."

And, on top of all that, Gen-Zers are the first to *Ohhhh!* and *Ahhhh!* when they hear or see something cute or precious.

In a day and age when tempers easily flare, folks bully and unfollow each other over even the slightest disagreements, and chaos runs rampant, Gen-Z's caring and passionate approach to cherishing the good things in life is a path we can all benefit from observing and following.

Finally, for further proof that Gen-Zers are a sentimental bunch, I suggest you do either the DIY Gen-Z Time Capsules project on page 207 or the Dear 5-Year-Old Me activity on page 211.

❝ Do I consider myself to be a sentimental person? Why or why not?

ASK A GEN-ZER

❝ Are you a sentimental person? Why or why not? Do you think your generation is overall a sentimental generation? Why or why not?

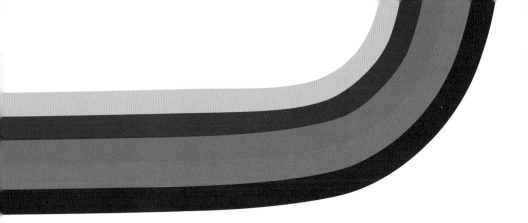

CHAPTER 49

JUST ASK THEM:
WHAT DOES THAT MEAN?

Here's a tip for proactively avoiding rolled eyes and a sarcastic "OK, BOOMER!" being tossed your way . . .

Learn to ask: "What does that mean?"

We and Gen-Z are in this life journey together, which means we are all teachers and students in ever-reversing roles. This is especially true when it comes to decoding Gen-Z speak. In fact, the terminology changes and transforms so quickly that if I wrote a few examples here they'd be dated and out of use by the time you read them.

This very helpful question also comes in handy when engaging Gen-Zers in important conversations, such as:

"What do all the letters, and the plus sign, in LGBTQIA+ mean?"

"What does anti-racist mean?"

"Who is [FILL IN THE BLANK WITH A CELEBRITY NAME YOU NEVER HEARD BEFORE]?"

Once when I was visiting with a class of Gen-Zers in Texas, and asking them a lot of questions as I tend to do, I was heartened to hear one student say that she welcomes it when people ask her questions, especially about being part of the LGBTQIA+ community, rather than jumping to conclusions and judgments.

Thoughtfully asking questions, without intending to mock or disdain the answer, doesn't show your age—it shows that you're interested and engaged, which is something Gen-Zers respect. (And if you still get an "OK, Boomer!" flung your way, it's best to just laugh and brush it off.)

66 **What is something I have heard Gen-Zers talking about that I didn't understand or have any clue about? Did I then ask them for an explanation? Why or why not?**

66 **What does _____ mean?**

CHAPTER 50

MANY OF THEM CARRY THE WEIGHT OF THE WORLD ON THEIR SHOULDERS

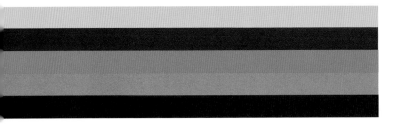

One time when I was chatting with a Gen-Zer, the conversation went something like this:

Me: "What do you want me to know about your generation?"

Gen-Zer: "That it's up to my generation to save the planet."

Me: "What do you mean?"

Gen-Zer: "Things like climate change especially are destroying the planet, and no one else is really doing anything about it. So it's up to us. And this constantly stresses me out!"

I paused. A discussion about climate change aside, I picked up on something much deeper here.

Me: "Why does climate change stress you out?"

Gen-Zer: "Because the media and my professors and other adults keep telling us how the world is going to end soon because of it or for other reasons, and that I need to do something to change it. And so I'm afraid the world as we know it will end and it'll be my fault."

Me: "Wow! But wait, it sounds like you are saying that you alone have to save the world. You shifted from you collectively as Gen-Z, which is a heavy thought already, to you individually. As if the weight of world, and its survival, is on your shoulders alone."

The Gen-Zer did not pause, did not even give hint of the slightest hesitation.

Gen-Zer: "That's right. I feel like I alone have to do something about climate change, or else the destruction of the planet and the loss of all those lives are on my hands alone. My friends all feel the same way."

I paused again, stunned and heartbroken, my head spinning.

Gen-Zer: "I think about this constantly, like every second of every day. And my anxiety about it never stops because I don't know what the ultimate solution is and anything I try to do is never enough to solve the larger problem."

I was really at a complete loss for words by this point, but still, I tried.

Me: "I hope you know that big issues like this one, and others, are not your responsibility alone. We are all in this together, no matter what comes our way as a planet."

Admittedly, my answer was insufficient—albeit true—but still a weak response in terms of the much more serious mental health impact I had just witnessed firsthand.

The Gen-Zer just looked at me—a melancholy gaze that haunts me even now as I recall our visit. This was one of the few times during my hundreds, if not thousands at this point, of encounters with Gen-Zers when I felt helpless. Yet, this experience also fueled my determination to help even more.

In recent years as the world has started to take notice of Gen-Zers, young people like the one above and how they feel about issues, such as climate change, have become the butt of very cruel stereotypes and jokes.

Years ago, when I would hear stories about young people believing that the world will soon end because of climate change, global conflicts, and other situations, I couldn't quite wrap my head around the reality of their feelings. When I heard of young people contemplating suicide and actually dying by suicide because the stress and pressure of these issues was too much to bear, I especially could not understand the why—specifically why they each personalize these issues so much.

But then my paths crossed with the Gen-Zer above, and many others since, and the conversation that followed about this topic helped me to better understand.

Their pain, stress, anxiety, depression, and suicidal ideation over issues like climate change—and the belief pounded into them that this all falls squarely on them alone to solve—is real. To super clarify: Gen-Zers do not only see big issues as a mission for their generation to solve—many of them deeply internalize and believe that they alone need to find the solution. That they alone, drenched by the weight and pull of a global quicksand, are solely responsible to save the planet or else be blamed for its demise for a lack of said solution.

This is the single biggest cautionary tale of our time because of the sheer force of the destruction and mental health impact it's currently having on Gen-Zers. The rotten roots of this mass pathology are within the answers to the following questions that the rest of us need to start seriously asking ourselves ASAP:

Who is directly, or even indirectly, telling young people today, or leading them to believe, that the world could end because of [FILL IN THE BLANK]? Am I?

What is the real motivation of the folks who are conveying this message to young people? Am I one of these purveyors of mass destruction?

What outcome do the folks conveying this message to young people hope to achieve?

What can the rest of us do to begin to change this perception that Gen-Zers have of themselves as the sole, all-or-nothing superheroes upon which the deafening fate of the world depends?

Where is the balance and optimism here, even when it comes to the most serious issues that we as local, national, and global communities face?

ASK YOURSELF

❝ Have I ever heard a Gen-Zer express that they feel a sole responsibility for the fate and survival of the world? Have I ever directly, or even indirectly, fueled this perception that many of them have?

ASK A GEN-ZER

❝ Do you feel responsible for saving the world when it comes to things like climate change, global conflicts, and other issues? If so, why do you feel that way? Where or who did that message originally come from?

CHAPTER 51

THEY HAVE EXACTLY WHAT IT TAKES TO BE FUTURE

WORLD LEADERS

What do we want in our leaders?

Honesty. Integrity. Resilience. Strength. Courage. Compassion. Humility. Strategy. Creativity. Intelligence. Love. Out-of-the-box thinking. Moral compasses. Innovation. Battle scars. Survivors. Understanding. Open minds. . . .

Go ahead, add whatever else you'd like to the list.

Whatever list you finally produce, I bet you can easily find a slate of Gen-Zers around you who match the description and who are up for the challenge.

They are the greatest hope and proof yet that the future is so bright!

But don't just take my word for it. To further explore what the future might look like, check out the It's A Gen-Z World, And We All Just Live In It! activity on page 215.

66 What qualities do I think a great leader should have? Do I see those qualities in young people?

ASK A GEN-ZER

66 Do you think you are a good leader? Why or why not? What qualities do you think a great leader should have? Do you see those qualities represented in yourself and your generation?

CHAPTER 52

DON'T TRY TO COM-PLETELY UNDERSTAND THEM—THAT'S

IMPOSSIBLE

Seriously, don't overthink this one.

Just take it for what it's worth, and don't be too hard on yourself when it comes to deciphering Gen-Zers.

66 **What is one main thing that I want to better understand about Gen-Zers?**

66 **What is one main thing that you wish older adults understood about you and your generation?**

ACTIVITY GUIDE

Since we all inhabit and navigate the Gen-Z Universe, getting to better know and understand these incredible young people interactively is always helpful. The following activities and projects can be easily adapted at home, school, a library, community organizations, a workplace, or anywhere else Gen-Zers are rocking the world with you.

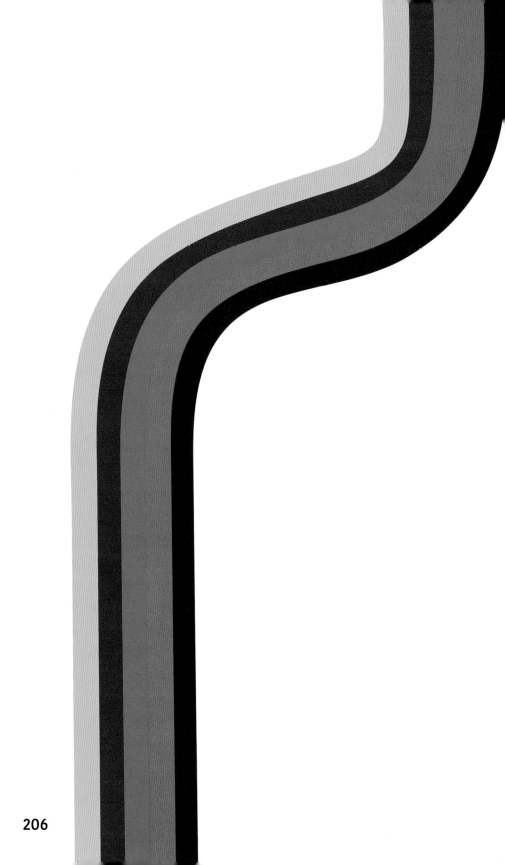

DIY Gen-Z Time Capsules

Inspired by the 610 *Time Capsules* that Andy Warhol had assembled in cardboard boxes, I kicked off one semester by handing each of my students a large manila envelope. I instructed them to fill their envelopes during the following four months. Just before finals week, everyone shared the contents of their first-year time capsules, shedding much light on who they are as individuals and collectively as a generation. This project eventually led to my collaboration with The Andy Warhol Museum to create *The Gen-Z Time Capsule*.

To create DIY Gen-Z Time Capsules with your Gen-Zers:

1. Give each Gen-Zer a large manila envelope with their name on it. If they'd like, they can further personalize their time capsule by decorating it. And, by the way, consider compiling your own personal time capsule to share with the Gen-Zers.

2. Choose a timeframe during which they will compile their time capsules: one month, four months, a year—whatever works best for you and them.

3. Tell them to place their time capsule somewhere convenient, visible, and accessible so they can frequently add items to it.

4. During the timeframe of this project, instruct them to add whatever items they would like to their time capsules, such as

photos, receipts, sketches, concert tickets, favorite collectibles, cards, favorite food wrappers, souvenirs from adventures, etc.

5. Once the timeframe for compiling the time capsules ends, as a group, have each Gen-Zer share and discuss the contents of their time capsule.

For more information about *The Gen-Z Time Capsule* project at The Andy Warhol Museum, please visit: https://www.warhol. org/timecapsule/time-capsules/

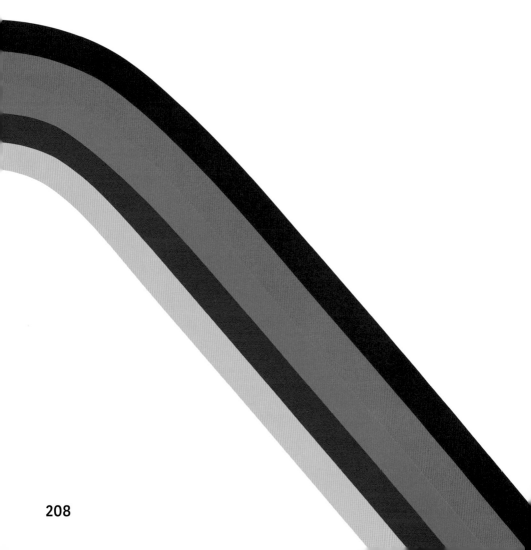

The Blank Sketchbook Project

One year, I handed my new students two blank sketch-books to be filled in during each class meeting throughout the semester. This activity came with only one rule: Nothing is off limits! Four months later, the sketchbooks were filled with their humor, fears, venting, scribbles, conversations, declarations, scriptures, F-bombs, favorite quotes, tic-tac-toe games, acronyms I had to Google, and, of course, the sketch of a penis that another student later modestly covered with masking tape (which made me chuckle and reminded me that while wise beyond their years, these students were still teens prone to mischief).

What ultimately emerged from this activity was a greater portrait of the many different layers that Gen-Zers embody.

To do The Blank Sketchbook Project with your Gen-Zers:

1. Purchase a sturdy, hardbound, blank sketchbook. Preferably one with a white cover, as they like to fill that in as well.

2. Depending on how often you meet with your Gen-Zers, choose a timeframe during which to do this project: one month, four months, a year—whatever works best for you and them.

3. Explain to the Gen-Zers that you will pass around the blank sketchbook during every group meeting, during which they can (anonymously) write, draw, scribble, paste/tape items, or add anything else they'd like.

I suggest that you be daring and follow my lead in telling them: Nothing is off limits!

4. Once the timeframe for the project ends, go through the filled sketchbook with the Gen-Zers and discuss the contents.

Dear 5-Year-Old Me

Over the years, one of the best and most impactful ways I have learned to get to know my Gen-Z students has been to ask them to write a letter to their 5-year-old selves. This project enables them to reflect and critically think about the journey they have had from their earliest memories to present day. For me, reading their letters always takes me directly into their hearts and minds in a way nothing else ever could.

To do the Dear 5-Year-Old Me letter-writing activity with your Gen-Zers:

1. You may have to first explain to them what a formal letter is, including what stationery is. In fact, this could be a great opportunity for you to help them create stationery that they can use not only for this activity but also for future letters they may send, including personal letters to family and friends as well as letters for internships and jobs.

The letters can be typed and printed, or handwritten. I always prefer handwritten, as our handwriting is one more glimpse into who we are as individuals.

2. Instruct them to think about their life journey from the time they were five or so years old until today—the joys and sorrows, the successes and the challenges, the good and the bad. Then, ask them to write a letter from themselves in present day telling their five-year-old selves what that journey to now will be like.

For the letters, give them the freedom to focus on summarizing the whole journey, honing in on a particular experience, or using any other content they'd like.

3. When the letters are completed, encourage the Gen-Zers to share their letters by either reading them aloud to the group, or passing them all around for the group to silently read and contemplate. Either way, I guarantee you will have a lot to discuss!

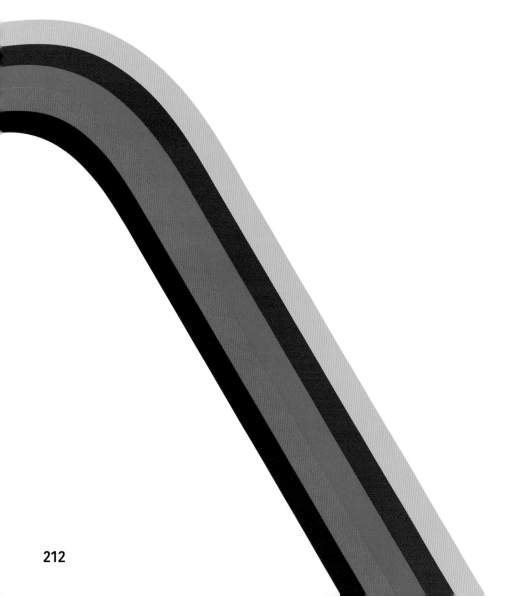

Dear 85-Year-Old Me

Here is some really promising news: Contrary to many stereotypes, most Gen-Zers do actually envision themselves growing old—in fact, very old!

Over the years, one of the best and most impactful ways I have learned to get to know my Gen-Z students has been to ask them to write a letter to their 85-year-old selves. This project enables them to reflect and critically think about the journey ahead—family, friends, hopes, dreams, careers, adventures, challenges, etc. For me, reading their letters always takes me directly into their hearts and imaginations in a way nothing else ever could.

To do the Dear 85-Year-Old Me letter-writing activity with your Gen-Zers:

1. You may have to first explain to them what a formal letter is, including what stationery is. In fact, this could be a great opportunity for you to help them create stationery that they can use not only for this activity but also for future letters they may send, including personal letters to family and friends as well letters for internships and jobs.

The letters can be typed and printed, or handwritten. I always prefer handwritten, as our handwriting is one more glimpse into who we are as individuals.

2. Instruct them to think about what their life journey ahead may look like—the joys and sorrows, the successes and the challenges,

the good and the bad. Then, ask them to write a letter from themselves in present day telling their eighty-five-year-old selves what that journey will be like.

For the letters, give them the freedom to focus on summarizing the whole journey, honing in on a particular experience, or using any other content they'd like.

3. When the letters are completed, encourage the Gen-Zers to share their letters by either reading them aloud to the group or passing them all around for the group to silently read and contemplate. Either way, I guarantee you will have a lot to discuss!

Also, encourage them to save their letters so they can read them when they really are eighty-five!

It's A Gen-Z World, And We All Just Live In It!

       Gen-Zers represent the future of our world, but what will that world look like? The best way to find out is to go directly to the source. This activity gives them an opportunity to dream, critically think, and build their vision of a future world, and have fun doing it. And it will give you a chance to learn more about their dreams, thoughts, priorities, and imaginations.

       To do the It's A Gen-Z World, And We All Just Live In It! activity with your Gen-Zers:

1. Use a very large sheet or banner of paper attached to a wall, or a chalk or dry-erase board. And gather whatever art supplies you want to use: markers, paints, crayons, colored pencils, etc. This project could also be created as a more permanent mural, if the right location is available.

2. Prepare your Gen-Zers for this activity by discussing what their vision of a future world includes, and their reasoning behind it.

3. Then, tell them that using the art supplies they are to draw the ideal Gen-Z-led city of the future on the mural. It can include anything they would like. Each Gen-Zer should then have the opportunity and time to add whatever elements they want to the mural. This activity can be done during one group gathering or over a longer period.

4. When the mural is completed, discuss it with your Gen-Zers.

5. Finally, consider displaying the mural in a place where other people can see it, in order for them to learn more about the dreams, creativity, and vision of Gen-Z, and to inspire their own imaginations and optimism about what the future could look like.

The Gen-Z Blackout Poetry Project

I was first introduced to blackout poetry through Austin Kleon's book *Newspaper Blackout*. To create blackout poetry, you first choose source materials, such as a newspaper or magazine article, a blog essay or listicle, a page from a book, or any other materials that have a significant amount of writing on them. Using a black marker, you then cover up, or black out, all the text you do not want, leaving only the words and phrases you do want that will form a poem, including the poem's title if you want.

This activity is a great way of sparking your Gen-Zers' imaginations and creativity, while also showing them just how cool the genre of poetry is!

To do The Gen-Z blackout poetry Project with your Gen-Zers:

1. Gather a collection of old newspapers, magazines, books, and/or other written materials, including printed-out blog essays or listicles. Also, have enough black markers for every Gen-Zer.

2. Explain to your Gen-Zers what blackout poetry is, and, if possible, show them examples—from Austin Kleon's book, on the internet, or samples you created.

3. If you want, either allow them to create poems about anything they'd like or set a theme, such as "My Life as a Gen-Zer."

4. Allow the Gen-Zers to peruse the source materials and choose the printed pieces of writing they would like to use.

5. Once they complete their blackout poems, have them share the poems by either reading them aloud to the group or passing them all around for the group to silently read and contemplate. Either way, fun and impactful discussions will flow from there!

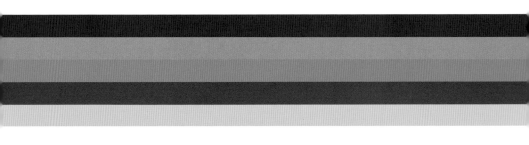

Pick A Word, Any Word

The simplicity of this activity will lead to some of the most insightful, inspiring, creative, fun, and impactful presentations and discussions you'll ever have with your Gen-Zers.

There are several ways you can approach this activity:

Option 1: Ask each Gen-Zer to choose one word that has meaning to them. Then, have them present the word and what it means to them to the group.

Option 2: Put a bunch of random words—that either you write or they write—in a bowl. Have each Gen-Zer choose one word from the bowl and then, via improv, talk about what that word means to them.

Option 3: For some cross-generational fun, have your Gen-Zers research the words, slang, and other jargon that are associated with the various generations listed on the next page.

The Generations Timeline

The Greatest Generation: People born before and in 1927.

The Silent Generation: People born between 1928 and 1945.

Baby Boomers: People born between 1946 and 1964.

Generation X: People born between 1965 and 1980.

Millennials: People born between 1981 and 1996.

Generation Z: People born between 1997 and 2012.

Generation Alpha: People born in 2013 and after.

Then, either have them choose a word to focus on or have them draw one of the words out of a bowl. Ask them to then research and present the word to the group, including what generation it's from, what it means, and what they personally think of it.

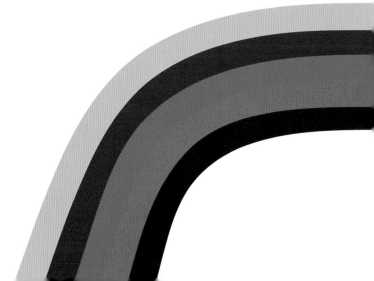

Pick A Topic, Any Topic

This activity will lead to some of the most insightful, inspiring, creative, fun, and impactful presentations and discussions you'll ever have with your Gen-Zers.

There are several ways you can approach this activity:

Option 1: Ask each Gen-Zer to choose one topic that has meaning to them. Then, have them present the topic and what it means to them to the group.

Option 2: Put a bunch of random topics—that either you write or they write—in a bowl. Have each Gen-Zer choose one topic from the bowl and then, via improv, talk about what that topic means to them.

Option 3: For some cross-generational fun, have your Gen-Zers research the topics and events that are associated with the various generations, and their eras, listed on the next page.

The Generations Timeline

The Greatest Generation: People born before and in 1927.The Silent Generation: People born between 1928 and 1945.

Baby Boomers: People born between 1946 and 1964.

Generation X: People born between 1965 and 1980.

Millennials: People born between 1981 and 1996.

Generation Z: People born between 1997 and 2012.

Generation Alpha: People born in 2013 and after.

Then, either have them choose a topic to focus on or have them draw one of the topics out of a bowl. Ask them to then research and present the topic to the group, including what generation it's from, what it means, and what they personally think of it.

The Gen-Z Brain Project

While I was a student at Harvard University Graduate School of Education, one of my favorite professors was Howard Gardner, who created the Theory of Multiple Intelligences. This is likely a theory—proposing that we all learn in different ways—that you have heard of and/or even utilize when working with young people.

Understanding that we all learn most effectively in different ways, and incorporating that understanding into the projects we assign and other activities we do with young people, will lead to some amazing and creative results and impactful learning.

For The Gen-Z Brain Project, the main focus will be on the brain, but the modes of creation and presentation will be left up to each individual Gen-Zer and how they process or choose to process the activity in the best way they can:

1. Tell your Gen-Zers that the topic for this activity is: The Brain. (Period. Just, the brain.)

2. They are to research and focus on any part or facet of the brain they'd like—anatomy, mental health, its relationship to the rest of the body, how it plays into our thinking or creativity, etc.

3. Explain that the final way in which their research is handed in or presented is also up to them. The following are a few options, but also invite them to combine these or to go in completely different and unique directions:

- Draw or paint a portrait, or create a collage, of your brain.
- Create a sculpture—from clay or found materials—of your brain.
- Write an essay or research paper about some facet of the brain.
- Create a piece of performance art about your brain.
- Write a poem or song about your brain.
- Create the concept for a video game about your brain.
- Write a letter to your brain.
- Present an invention idea, and explain what parts of your brain you'll need to create it and why.

The Gen-Z Tree Project

There is a beautiful Greek proverb that reads: *A society grows great when old men and women plant trees in whose shade they will never sit.*

Every generation leaves many of these metaphorical, and literal, trees for future generations to embrace, enjoy, learn from, grow from, and build upon. This is certainly already true with Gen-Z and the impact they are having on mental health advocacy, anti-racism, LGBTQIA+ issues, and so much more.

To do The Gen-Z Tree Project with your Gen-Zers:

1. Present this Greek proverb to your Gen-Zers, and discuss what it means—both generally and, to them, personally and collectively as a generation. Also, ask them to reflect on the metaphorical trees that other generations planted for them and that their generation is already planting for the future.

2. Then, depending on where your group meets, you can plant an actual tree or adopt an existing tree that is nearby, and call it The Gen-Z Tree (even add a plaque by the tree, if possible). During your meetings together, you can visit your Gen-Z Tree, watching it grow, discussing how it is changing, and circling the conversation back to Gen-Z and what this all means to them and for them, and for the world.

Or, if planting or adopting a tree is not possible, ask your Gen-Zers to artistically create their own (individual or collectively together) original Gen-Z Tree—by drawing, painting, or sculpting it, assembling a collage of it, or using any other creative medium they'd like, including poetry, songwriting, or performance art.

When the Gen-Z Trees are completed, have the Gen-Zers present each of their trees to the class, and discuss them. And, if feasible, publicly display the trees for others to see and learn from them.

The Gen-Z Reality Show

I always have so much fun doing this project with my students. Since a prevailing stereotype is that they all just want to be famous (which is so not true!), it's entertaining to let them stretch their imaginations and strategize what going Hollywood might look like.

To do The Gen-Z Reality Show activity with your Gen-Zers:

1. Divide them into manageable groups of about four to six members each. Each group becomes a production team.

2. The mission for each production team is to create a concept and outline for an inspirational and motivational reality show that would star Gen-Zers their age and be set somewhere that Gen-Zers frequent—school, library, community center, gym, hometown, neighborhood, etc. (Preferably somewhere that they personally know well so they can easily envision it.)

3. They can choose whether their reality show will be a competition series (with games and challenges, and eliminations and an ultimate champion) or a docuseries (that follows a group of Gen-Zers and shows their lives).

4. Each production team will outline the format (competition or docuseries), the cast (what personality types of Gen-Zers will be cast for the show and why), what competitions or activities will be showcased in the series, and what positive mes-

sages or lessons they aim to present within the context of their reality show.

5. Once the production strategies and plans are crafted, each production team will present their show idea to the larger group.

Name That Generation Game

The more we learn and understand about other individuals, groups, and generations, the more we tend to learn and understand about ourselves.

For this cross-generational game, it's time to see just how much Gen-Zers know about other generations. Even if the answer is not that much, then they are about to learn a lot, and have fun doing it.

To play the Name That Generation Game with your Gen-Zers:

1. Using the generations timeline on the next page—either you alone or as a group—research the history that took place during each generational era. Choose as many historical facts from each generational era as you wish and write them on separate pieces of paper without the related generation listed (but be sure to keep a separate answer key).

The Generations Timeline

The Greatest Generation: People born before and in 1927.

The Silent Generation: People born between 1928 and 1945.

Baby Boomers: People born between 1946 and 1964.

Generation X: People born between 1965 and 1980.

Millennials: People born between 1981 and 1996.

Generation Z: People born between 1997 and 2012.

Generation Alpha: People born in 2013 and after.

2. To play the game, divide your Gen-Zers into teams. Then, have each team pull a historical fact out of a bowl. In a designated amount of time, they must name what generational era the event or fact is from. If they give the correct answer, they get a point. If they are wrong, they get no point. At the end of the game, the team with the most points wins.

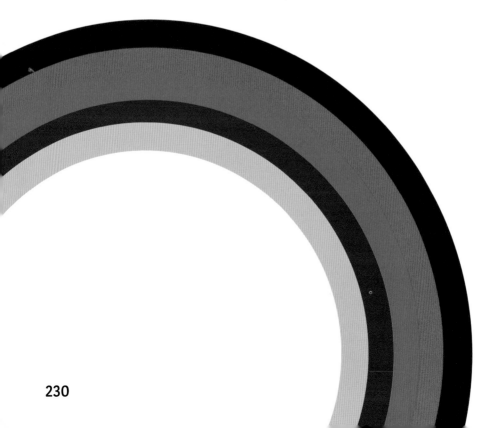

The Planting Truth Project

Gen-Zers have turned tearing down stigmas and debunking stereotypes into an art form. In speaking their truths loudly and clearly, they are planting and cultivating those many truths across the globe. So, in that spirit, I created The Planting Truth Project below.

To do The Planting Truth Project with your Gen-Zers:

1. As a group, list as many stigmas and stereotypes as you all can think of—about Gen-Z, mental health, race, LGBTQIA+, and/or any other political or social issues you'd like to include.

2. Then, discuss each of the stigmas and stereotypes, talking about why they exist and what is wrong about them. This may include, and require, research.

3. Next, have each group member choose one or more stigmas/stereotypes. For each stigma/stereotype, give them a small piece of paper, 3" x 3" or 4" x 4". Instruct them to write "Stigma" or "Stereotype" at the top of one side of the paper, and beneath it they should write the stigma or stereotype they chose. On the other side of the paper, they should write "The Truth" at the top, and beneath it write the fact about why the stigma or stereotype is wrong.

4. To plant the truths, find a place outside individually or as a group, dig a hole or holes, and bury/plant the slips of paper. Or, using small pots (one per group member), soil, and seeds/plants/

flowers, the papers can be placed on the bottom of the pots, filled with the dirt and seeds/plants/flowers, and then taken home. This can also be done by placing all the slips of paper on the bottom of one large pot, covering them with soil and seeds/plants/flowers, and then watching the plants or flowers grow together as a group.

Gen-Z Show-And-Tell

One of my favorite ways to get to know my students and help them get to know each other at the start of a school year or semester is to have them interview each other, with a fun show-and-tell. However, this activity could be done at any time during your work with Gen-Zers.

To do the Gen-Z Show-And-Tell activity with your Gen-Zers:

1. Divide your group into pairs (including a group of three, if you have an odd number of young people). Each Gen-Zer in the pair will be both interviewer and interviewee.

2. Instruct the pairs to talk and find out five or so interesting things about each other. They should then translate that information into three or so personalized questions that they can ask each other on presentation day.

3. Also, for presentation day, ask everyone to bring in one item that is special to them for show-and-tell.

4. On presentation day, arrange two chairs at the front of the room. While sitting in the chairs, each pair will ask one another the interview questions and answer them.

5. The interviews will conclude by having each pair share their show-and-tell items.

6. Each pair's interviews can then be followed by questions from the group and further discussion.

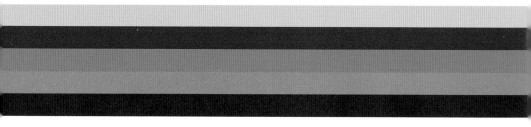

The Intersections Of Gen-Z

Each one of us is a glorious maze of intersections—crisscrossing physical, social, political, and cultural identities, traits, beliefs, and interests; some permanent, some ever-evolving— that ultimately creates the unique and dynamic person we are. These infinite combinations, and their potential for good, include racial identity, gender identity, faith, politics, social issues, hobbies, jobs, dreams, physical and mental health, talents, where we live, and so much more.

Critically thinking about, contemplating, and understanding the many pathways and journeys that intersect within us helps us to better understand ourselves, each other, and the world around us.

To do The Intersections Of Gen-Z activity with your Gen-Zers:

1. On blank sheets of paper, have each Gen-Zer write down every identity, trait, belief, or interest about themselves (that they are comfortable sharing): racial identity, gender identity, favorite subject, hobbies, career goals, faith, sports, beliefs, opinions, physical and mental challenges, talents, hometowns, etc.

2. Then, on other blank sheets of paper, have them start writing those identities, traits, beliefs, and interests so that the words somehow intersect with each other—two or more intersecting identities/traits/beliefs/interests at a time, or one large maze of all the words crisscrossing and intersecting with each other.

For example, for one particular student, "race" and "poetry" may intersect in that they process feelings and understandings, and challenges, about their specific race via the poetry they write. Therefore, on this sheet of paper they would write the two words intersecting over the common "e" in both words like you might see in a crossword puzzle. Or, sans a common letter between words, the student could simply and even creatively layer the words over each other in some other way.

As an alternative, hang a giant blank mural in your meeting space and have all the Gen-Zers add their many intersections to that one space, even crisscrossing and intersecting with each other's additions.

3. Finally, have the Gen-Zers share and/or present, and discuss, what they learned from the activity about themselves and about each other. A powerful outcome here will be when your Gen-Zers see how each of their own individual intersections cross paths with the intersections of others in the group and beyond.

A----->Gen-Z

Since the main goal here is to get to know Gen-Zers better—literally everything from A to Z—and since they are good and speedy at thinking on their feet, you can have a little fun putting that quick wit to the test. And doing it old school with a handwritten ABCs twist.

To do the A----->Gen-Z activity with your Gen-Zers:

1. Give each Gen-Zer a piece or two of blank paper. On the paper, have them each write the letters of the alphabet going down the left-hand side of the page.

2. Instruct them that within a certain timeframe—two, five, ten minutes, or whatever other time span you want to use with the help of a stopwatch—they are to race through the alphabet writing one thing that they like (it can be anything: food, fashion, video games, slang, sports, names of family or friends, celebrities, movies or TV shows, etc.) that begins with each letter. Ideally, just one word, name, title, or phrase per letter.

3. Once time is up, ask them to share their lists with the group, maybe focusing on one or two entries. Or the lists can be passed around for the group to silently read and contemplate. It will be cool to compare and contrast, and to gain more insight into who Gen-Zers are, as individuals and collectively as a generation.

Acknowledgments

First and foremost, huge thanks to every Gen-Zer with whom I have crossed paths during the past several years! Each of our interactions was key to crafting and sharing this book with the world so that others can get to know you all better, as individuals and as one of the most incredible generations in history. To all the other Gen-Zers around the world, I look forward to our paths eventually crossing. I am always and forever your #1 fan!

To the extraordinary team at Familius, who enthusiastically embraced this book and its mission from day one, much gratitude! Especially Founder and President Christopher Robbins (who is "Dad" to several Gen-Zers!); my editor and book designer, Mckay Rappleyea (who *is* a Gen-Zer!); the Marketing, PR, and Sales team, including Jaiden Wong, Ashley Mireles, Adina Oberman; and the countless others who are responsible for getting this book into your hands.

To my agent Katherine Odom-Tomchin and the team at Folio Literary Management, who always have my back on this incredible journey, and who love Gen-Zers as much as I do, a million thanks!

And I extend a very special and celebratory round of applause to ALL OF YOU—parents, teachers, coaches, librarians, community organizers, employers, and anyone else who is currently navigating the Gen-Z Universe. ROCK ON! +++++

About the Author

John Schlimm, Harvard-trained educator, artist, advocate, and international award-winning author, was among the first to start piecing together the authentic and multifaceted face of Generation Z—beyond the stigmas, stereotypes, and often misguided media profiling of these dynamic young people, who remain largely misunderstood and vastly underestimated.

During the past several years, John's extensive, revealing work and trusted relationship with Gen-Zers across the country has resulted in several thought-provoking essays—for *Huffington Post, Harvard Ed. Magazine,* and others—and his groundbreaking collaboration with The Andy Warhol Museum to create *The Gen-Z Time Capsule,* which is a participatory project helping Gen-Zers to further introduce themselves to the world—including to their own parents, teachers, community leaders, employers, and others—while also turning them into a bona fide work of Pop Art.

Connect with John on social media here:
Instagram: @johnschlimm
Facebook: www.facebook.com/JohnSchlimm
Twitter: @JohnSchlimm
Snapchat: @JohnSchlimm
Website: www.JohnSchlimm.com

About Familius

Visit Our Website: www.familius.com

Familius is a global trade publishing company that publishes books and other content to help families be happy. We believe that the family is the fundamental unit of society and that happy families are the foundation of a happy life. We recognize that every family looks different, and we passionately believe in helping all families find greater joy. To that end, we publish books for children and adults that invite families to live the Familius Ten Habits of Happy Family Life: *love together, play together, learn together, work together, talk together, heal together, read together, eat together, give together,* and *laugh together.* Founded in 2012, Familius is located in Sanger, California.

Connect
Facebook: www.facebook.com/familiustalk
Twitter: @familiustalk, @paterfamilius1
Pinterest: www.pinterest.com/familius
Instagram: @familiustalk

FAMILIUS
Helping families be happy.

The most important work you ever do will be within the walls of your own home.